L
O
S
E
R

by Russell Clark

Cover Design by John Lee

Praise for LOSER

"There's a scene in the movie Dead Poets Society, *where professor John Keating asks his English lit students to stand up on their desks to give them a different perspective on life. Former pastor Russell Clark does that for the little Methodist church he led in tiny Reddick, Fla., starting a three-year revolution there that soon had his suddenly exploding congregation featured on the United Methodist webpage for having "the secret to church growth." Clark gets it. He understands, unlike so many ministers mired in the same old ritualistic rut, that sometimes following Jesus means getting down into the mess, even if it comes with a heavy price. God bless him for reminding us of that in* Loser."
- Jim Reeves, retired award-winning sports columnist and author of Dallas Cowboys: Legends of America's Team.

*"*Loser *by Russell Clark is nothing short of a present-day update of John Bunyan's* Pilgrim's Progress. *It is a post-modern romp with God, our companion on the way to discovering the messy, wonderful, OWESOME* truth about ourselves, our relationships, our failures and successes, and grace powerful enough to see us through all the day long and all the night through. When the Prophet Isaiah invented "Immanuel" to name the God of his hopes and dreams, someone like Russell Clark discovered in the shambles of his early ministry is what Isaiah had in mind. So, settle back, prepare to laugh. Prepare to find hope breaking out in your version of a small-town Florida Church. And prepare to get messy with the people "Immanuel," "God-With-Us" is sending your way.*

Loser *is a pilgrimage of wonder and hope. So, put on your traveling shoes, and go with Rev. Clark. Go through the mud until you find out that the glorious, muddy journey is really what God-With-Us had in mind for you and me all along. OWESOME*!*

*See the definition given in the book. Then dare to get excited about it."
- Dr. Stephen V. Sprinkle, professor at Brite Divinity School and author of Unfinished Lives: Reviving the Memories of LGBTQ Hate Crimes Victims.

"Russell Clark reminds us that our story is intertwined with God's story. His writing lifts up "ordinary moments where God has turned (our lives) into something extraordinary." His honest and forthright ability to share the unconditional love of God, while also affirming the need for perseverance in the messiness of life allows Clark to do two things at the same time: draw on his narrative in creative and substantive ways while also illuminating God's grace at the most profound level. This is ultimately the good news of Clark's work and the manner in which he engages the reader. Through his life and stories the reader

sees the power of love as Clark affirms that there are "moments . . . set apart as something meaningful," and that makes all the difference."

- Dr. Joretta L. Marshall, dean at Brite Divinity School and author of How Can I Forgive?: A Study of Forgiveness

"He came to us much like Elijah to the Hebrew children: a flash of lightning and a clap of thunder right out of the darkness. We needed him and he needed us. Russell writes from the heart -- and what a big heart it is. A heart he wears right out where everyone can see it. There were moments for me in the book where tissues weren't enough for the emotion I felt. There is no doubt Russell loves you and you -- just like us in Reddick -- will love him too."

- Jim Stroup, Mayor of Reddick, Florida and Lay Leader of the First United Methodist Church in Reddick, Florida

"I'm often haunted by the reality that bad things happen to good people. This is one of those stories. However, it doesn't end there. In this book, the author describes his journey of becoming an exiled loser to becoming a winner at life. If you've ever had a major disappointment in your life, this read can provide some mile markers toward healing."

- Joe Carmichael, Retired United Methodist Pastor

"It is God's friendship to us in the middle of our messes that affirms we are indeed loved—no strings attached. Through the story he is living as a disciple of Jesus, and his experience and history as a people's pastor, Russell's life story details a God that is not disconnected from his Creation, but rather compellingly intertwined throughout the details of our lives, in love. Loser sets the table of communion for those of us who find ourselves exercising our faith while living in the cross-section of faith and doubt."

- Andrew Greer, multiple Dove Award-nominated singer/songwriter and author of Transcending Mysteries: Who is God, and What Does He Want from Us?

LOSER
by Russell Clark

<u>Table of Contents:</u>

Booking Information – P.153

Introduction:
Ordinary Loser

"Your life is too boring to write a story about it."

An encouraging college professor once told me this.

And she was right.

This isn't an extraordinary story. There isn't some "Come to Jesus" moment.

This is an ordinary story about a former preacher who is not "saved."

//

My wife and I were grocery shopping one day when we lived in Florida and my phone rang.

"Russell, what's happening?! This is Buddy."

Buddy was the Baptist preacher whose church was next door to the church where I was serving as pastor in Reddick, FL. Buddy was a former drug addict, had tattoos up & down his arms, refused to wear anything but jeans to preach in, and immediately introduced rock music to his small town church. I loved him as soon as I met him.

"Buddy, what's up?!"

"Do you remember that strange man who visited your church?"

"Yes. The one who told me gay people are going to hell."

"Yep, that's the one. Well, he's been attending my church for a while and I had to tell him to leave my church because he was becoming a disruption. In our Sunday School class, he would hijack the class and try to express his points of view to the point of completely disrespecting every member of my church. So, I told him if he was going to continue to act like that he couldn't come back."

"Oh no. Well, that doesn't surprise me."

"But before he left he had something else to say. He told me we need to pray for the Methodist preacher next door."

"For me?"

"Yes. He said, 'Did you know the Methodist preacher isn't saved?'"

Hysterical laughter spewed out of me in the middle of the grocery store. I was laughing so hard my wife told me to calm down because I was causing a scene.

"That's hilarious! He was never satisfied with my salvation story because I didn't have a good enough 'Come to Jesus' moment."

//

This strange man confronted me after visiting our church at a Mother's Day event. He didn't pull any punches. He introduced himself and then immediately asked me the most controversial question in the church today:

"What are your thoughts on homosexuality?"

He asked the wrong pastor. He wasn't going to get the answer he wanted. I told him I believed homosexuals are God's children and God calls me to love God's children and guide them to be who they are called to be. But I'm not the one to tell people how to live; I'm the one to guide people to be who *God* sees them becoming.

"But do you think homosexuality is a sin?"

"As a matter of fact, I don't. But whether we, as Christians, do or not we're called to *love first* and *show grace first*. And I have many homosexual friends that I will go to bat for and be an advocate for so they experience this love like I have."

This led him to question my salvation.

//

I can't remember that one moment the heavens opened up and God took over my body like some possessed body snatcher. Probably because I think that's ridiculous.

There were numerous ordinary moments where God saved my life. These moments of amazing grace.

When I was in 6th grade, I received the "grand prize" for my essay on "Why I Want to Be a Christian." For a loser like me, this was life-changing. I never felt like I amounted to anything and this was the first time I felt like my life meant something. (Looking back, maybe it's not best to reward children for this because that means you make other children feel like their thoughts on being a Christian aren't good enough.)

Then I told the strange man about how mission trips changed my life. Mission trips were the time we went to serve others and each other and have fun doing it for an entire week. These trips brought me closer to God more than any other time.

On mission trips I was free to let loose and be myself – my true self, who God made me to be. My friends and I wore funny hats, we got kicked out of Walmart for getting on the intercom, and we set off fireworks illegally. And amidst all this rebellious, teenage behavior God was present teaching us that true worship is loving God and loving people in the dirty, messy places such as this.

I reflected back to my strange friend: "You know, I can't remember the one time I initially said, 'God, save me. I need you,' but there have been many, many times throughout my life like confirmation and mission trips that have been experiences of God's salvation."

I don't have that one extraordinary salvation story.

In fact, it's not really about being "once saved, always saved." Life is a journey of continuously being saved by God as we are awakened every day to God's grace and love despite the sin and suffering in this world.

There have been countless ordinary moments where God has turned my life into something extraordinary. Ordinary moments of grace when God has shown me more joy and peace and love in this life than I deserve. And it's for those moments that I keep on living. It's those not-so-boring moments I celebrate – whether or not the strange man or my encouraging professor think they make a good enough story to tell.

//

I laugh every time I remember hearing from the Baptist preacher that my story isn't a good enough salvation story for the strange man who met me *once*. Whenever I see Buddy, I remind him to keep praying for my "salvation."

I'm certainly an ordinary loser.

My life has been pretty boring. Much too boring to write a story about it.

But I know a God who's not boring.

9

Chapter 1:
Left Out

Professor Charles Xavier: "You know, I believe that true focus lies somewhere between rage and serenity. Would you mind if I..... [Charles makes a gesture to request permission to read Erik's mind]?

Erik Lehnsherr (Magneto): [Erik signals approval and while Charles reads Erik's mind we see moments of Erik's childhood with his mother.] What did you just do to me?

[Both Erik and Charles are crying.]

Professor Charles Xavier: I accessed the brightest corner of your memory system. It's a beautiful memory, Erik. Thank you.

Erik Lehnsherr (Magneto): I didn't know I still had that.

Professor Charles Xavier: There is so much more to you than you know. Not just pain and anger. There is good, too. I felt it. When you can access all of that, you will possess a power no one can match. Not even me.[1]

//

Growing up I played left out. I'm not talking about playing an outfielder in left field; I'm talking about being left out because I was terrible at sports. Every sport. Left out was my general position in soccer, baseball, football, you name it.

This left me to be teased for my lack of sports skills. I would get knocked down and made fun of. My nickname was "Russell with no muscles." My only saving grace was being a bully to the one kid who was more of a putz than me. At football practice one day, I pushed him down to gain the appreciation of the cool kids – to feel like less of a loser.

In a flash his dad was in my face and yanked my shoulder pads tightly.

"You little asshole! Don't ever do that to my son again!"

Well, that worked out well. Of course I'm the one to get caught and have a dad spitting in my face. I was left out from even my attempt to be a bully. I had no chance to beat the bullies at their own game.

//

As a young youth minister, I once stood up to a pastor I felt was a bully. She referred to herself as "The Bitch" because she knew she was difficult to work with and she was unapologetic about it. I felt as if she didn't respect me and often talked down to me. One second she would be as sweet as can be and then in the next moment she would turn on me – micromanaging and criticizing everything I did. It felt as if she was bipolar. Every other pastor I had worked for I referred to as Pastor but she demanded to be known as The Boss.

After two years of working for her and witnessing seven staff members leave during that tenure, I felt I didn't have integrity if I didn't expose how she treated people. I tried to get a job as a youth minister at another church but that pastor told me he couldn't hire me because he was afraid of her being mad at him. He'd had run-ins with her before, too. (This wouldn't be the last time The Bitch would be the reason I couldn't get a job.)

Standing up to a bully didn't work for me because she got promoted to District Superintendent.

I got my hand slapped for not respecting authority.

//

In Netflix's *Orange is the New Black*, a former nun stands up to an injustice she experiences and she is greeted with cheers from the other prisoners. She arrogantly soaks in their screams with pride. A prison guard who is watching the nun's reaction to being treated like a rock star asks an inmate, "Whatever happened to humility? Isn't that a virtue or something?"

Her response: *"One of the highest. People in power are always saying so."*[2]

Bullies have a way of getting what they want and leaving many of us losers in the fetal position.

Scared to move forward. Scared to stand up to bullies any longer.

And we call it humility.

//

In 6th grade, one of the first bullies I ever had once put his hands around my neck and pinned me up against the wall, my legs dangling above the floor in the middle of the classroom. He had been a bully to me for years before that moment.

I could actually see his house from my backyard. It was grey, lifeless, nothing intriguing about it. I walked past it every day on my way home from school. Well, usually I ran past it.

One day I remember bolting past him and a few of his bully buddies, running past his house to make it home to mine.

Someone told me my bully had an abusive father. To this day I don't know if that was true. They could have just told me that to make me feel better about getting bullied. Maybe so I would show compassion to the kid trying to take my life from me up against the wall.

To keep me humble as I struggled to breathe.

But thinking that changed me – to stop seeing his house and being filled with fear. But to see his house and pray for the boy living inside who was being hurt and thus chose to hurt others to numb his pain.

//

As I got older, new bullies like The Bitch came into my life. These bullies would attack in more subtle ways than a chokehold. But I would always learn something about why they acted the way they did. Sometimes abuse from a parent, sometimes anger towards God led them to treat others poorly, but always there was an underlying reason for them belittling and hurting me. Even The Bitch had reasons from her past that caused her to act the way she did.

I talked to a mentor about her. I told him I was so angry for what this bully did to me that I didn't know how to get rid of this anger. I will never forget his response:

"But Russell, you have every right to be angry. This person threatened every aspect of your life. She has threatened your marriage, your ministry, your career, everything you care about. You should be angry!"

We're taught as children to control our tempers. I had a bad temper in 5th and 6th grade, due in part to not knowing how to deal with being bullied. I would bang my head against the locker, turn over desks, anything to release frustration.

This moment with my mentor was the first time in my life I was told not to suppress my anger.

It's like when the angry superhero, The Hulk, embraced his greenness. For those unfamiliar with the story, Bruce Banner was a skinny scientist. When he becomes angry, he turns into this green monster who destroys everything in his path. The Hulk is a popular superhero for this very reason.[3]

We desire to let our anger out! We want to smash things when we're bullied! We want to stand up to injustice that happens to us and those around us!

14

We listen to rap and rock music because these artists understand our need to fully express how we feel. Rap music was birthed from black men needing a raw, poetic release of the injustices they experienced. Rap music is still extremely popular because it is a way to agitate the authorities and bullies who aren't treating us as we should be treated. It's getting angry because you know life can be better than this. It should be better!

"Hulk SMASH!"

Instead of repressing my green anger, I can let it all out! What a concept. To use my anger.

I can't tell you how many times I've talked to those who have just lost a family member and they were told to suppress their anger. Dealing with grief introduces a whole array of emotions and it is a total disservice to deny them. And that includes anger!

Let it all out!

We should be angry!

Trauma from a job loss or a death in the family or being disrespected requires a release. What do we do with this confusing situation, this unanswerable question?

Why in the hell did this happen to me?!

When a friend told me she lost her father and her friends told her not to be angry with God, I was quick to respond:

"Of course you should be angry! Your dad died! Death is confusing and it hurts. If there is *anyone* who you should be able to express your anger at, it is God. God can handle your anger and tears and frustration. Your anger at God is not a sign of a *lack* of faith. It is a sign *of faith* because it shows you are upset that things did not go the way you thought they should and you need God to restore some sort of order amidst this chaos. Your talking to God is much better than avoiding God and not asking for help.

"Get angry! Yell at God! *God can handle your anger!* It's okay to be angry!"

If a preacher ever tries to quote Luke 4:12 at you which says, "Do not put the Lord your God to the test,"[4] may you remind him/her that the book of Psalms[5] is full of people of faith crying out to God in frustration. And in the book of Job[6], Job's cries of agony are never seen as a lack of faith, but as a sign that he believes his present suffering is not the end.

Jesus became angry constantly. He called the leading religious leaders of his day "Sons of hell." He turned over tables when they were using churches as a marketplace instead of a place of worship. Jesus did not hide his anger. Anger is not a sin, but Jesus channeled his anger in appropriate ways.[7]

Anger is an emotion that we all feel at times and the first step to peace is to learn that it is okay to be angry.

In The Hulk's story, he witnessed his father kill his mother right in front of him in a fit of rage.[8] Of course any kid would have anger building inside of him after witnessing something so horrific.

This anger will not go away if we don't deal with it. If we bury it down and don't let it out in healthy ways, it is going to come up when we least expect it.

How many times have we yelled at our loved ones over a bad day that they didn't cause? The last time you lost your cool in the grocery line or flipped off that guy in traffic what really caused you to turn green with anger?

If we have a problem with someone and we don't deal with it, the problems are going to build up until they eventually explode – and at an inappropriate time.

It is okay to be angry. But the next step is to learn how to use our anger appropriately.

We must get to the root of why we are angry and deal with it. Sometimes this takes some long conversations with counselors, pastors, close friends, and family members. Sometimes this takes seeking reconciliation with the person or persons we're truly angry with.

Most importantly, after my mentor told me it was okay to be angry, he followed up this statement with a question,

"Now, what will you do with this anger?"

That's the question I've been trying to answer. That's the question of dealing with injustice in the pursuit of true justice.

That is as Frederich Nietzsche explains:

"Whoever fights monsters should see to it that he/she does not become one."[9]

If we're going to stand up to bullies, we must ensure we don't become a bully ourselves.

In *X-men: First Class*, the wise Professor Charles Xavier is trying to help his friend Erik (AKA – Magneto) to embrace his superpower. Charles can read Erik's mind and feelings and can see how Magneto's superpower comes from a place of anger. Charles knows that to embrace Erik's full potential he must find his power from that "place between rage and serenity."[10]

Peace lies somewhere between contentment (serenity) and discontentment (rage). Like Erik, we have this power inside of us fueled by discontentment – our anger towards how we know things *can* be, this passion for justice. And then there is another part to us – contentment – where we find shalom (wholeness) in seeing the reasons in our life we should be thankful for, the reasons we get up in the morning, the ordinary moments that have been life-changing for us.

Content with the way things are + Discontent with how we know they can be = Peace

St. Augustine puts it this way:

"Hope has two beautiful daughters. Anger at the way things are, and Courage to see to it that they don't remain the way they are."[11]

How can I find that place where my anger for bullies and my calmness/peace intersect? I must not lose this anger for those who drag us down and treat us like we're nothing, for those who use their power to belittle us and impose injustices upon us. But I also must not forget my call to have compassion for others. As Jesus taught, we can love our enemies and see the true spirit of those who hurt us. After all, Jesus loves the bullies, too.[12]

//

I wish I could say bullies learn not to be bullies. But they often stay the same. Your compassion for your bully does not mean they will change. The only one who can change is you. Find your peace.

I wish I could say bullies don't rise in power. But they do. Whatever tactics they used to make you feel less-than, they know how to use this power on others so they can rise to the top of the food chain. But there is a superpower in you too. I know it.

I wish I could say bullies can be defeated. But they can't. Bullies remain. They're a thorn in our side that come in different ways throughout our lives. Even bullies from our past often come back to haunt us when we hear horror stories of others going through the same ordeal.

They're triggers waiting to be pulled and they get in our heads and hearts again. *But we can change our perspective and stop giving them power over our lives.*

What will we do with this anger?

Do we direct our anger at the bully?
Or the father who abused him?
Or the father who called us assholes?
Or the coaches for making me play left out?
Or at myself for not knowing how to rise above the bully and escape his chokehold?

Or at the teachers, leaders, and authorities who didn't put a system in place to stop bullying from happening?
Or at *God* for allowing bullies to exist and *thrive* in our society?

Why, God, did you let this happen?!

When we start asking these questions it becomes less about the bully and more about where to direct our anger for the most good.

Do we seek justice? Even Martin Luther King Jr. recognized that the road to justice is longer than we could ever have imagined.[13] And he was assassinated in his pursuit for justice.

Do we crawl in a cave and pretend the outside world and the constant pain of others being bullied doesn't exist? I've tried this and it has only led me to let my anger out in unhealthy ways.

Do we make a maniacal plan to get revenge? Do we go green like the Hulk and smash our way out of the injustices that have embarked upon us? Then we leave the whole world in a pit of destruction.

Do we forgive our bully? One of my seminary professors, Dr. Joretta Marshall, once said, "It takes as long to forgive an act committed upon us as the length of time we spent having it done to us."[14] If you spent 20 years in an abusive relationship, chances are it might take you 20 years to move on from such a long time of thinking you're something you're not. Hearing abusive words and feeling the punch of abusive persons takes time to heal. The longer the external and internal bruises were made, the longer it takes to forgive the one who bruised us. Because no one knows but us how much the pain still hurts.

I think a bigger question to ask ourselves is:

How can I use this anger as a fire, a drive to do what's right and good and true? How can I achieve the most joy for not only myself but others who are being bullied?

And yes, even my bully can know there is another way to live if they ever choose to listen.

19

In *The Avengers*, Bruce Banner (The Hulk) says, "You want to know my secret? I'm always angry."[15]

The greatest disservice we can do to injustice and cruelty and sin and all the things that truly make us angry is to be apathetic and continue allowing ourselves and others to remain in that chokehold.

To not be angry at injustice and suffering is just as evil as what's being done to us.

I've seen anger turned into projects like Relay for Life or Stand up to Cancer. We've seen anti-bullying projects or the "It Gets Better" videos on YouTube. [16]

Fight off what angers you with love and inspiration and creativity and peace and joy. Channel your anger to change the world. Use your anger as strength to make sure what happened to you doesn't happen to anyone else, or at least to comfort those who are going through the same thing as you.

Find that place between anger and serenity where you can release your superpower.

If any of you have seen *The Matrix*, at the end of the movie Neo, the central character, starts to realize the world around him is more than meets the eye. He doesn't have to fight off his attacker anymore because he sees the world differently. He can move at ease to fight off bullets and punches because his attacker no longer has power. He's more aware of the truth to this world and how he can rise above it. There's more than meets the eye. [17]

There's more than the real world right in front of me. There's more than that chokehold of my attacker or his abusive father or his anger or my anger. There's something else going on.

Beyond the chokehold. Beyond my anger. Beyond my bully.

There is another world. The really real world. There's a different perspective and a purpose that comes with it.

There's a purpose for that anger. There's a reason to use that anger for good, for love, for forgiveness.

To bring peace in ways no one has thought of before. In ways no one has allowed us to think.

Like Neo learns in the movie, "There is no spoon."

There is no bully.
There is no chokehold.
There is no abusive father.
There is no manipulative boss.
There is no belittling authority.
There is no racism or religious judgment or radical terrorism.
There is no injustice.

Because these things no longer have power over my life.

There's a way to step beyond all this pain and suffering.

And see.

The bigger picture.

The place where our anger – our need for justice – and serenity meet.

There are children of God.
There are people who need your superpower.
There are those who need to know it gets better.
There are kids looking at you to see what you will do next.
There are losers like you who need to know there's a way to change this pain into gain.
There is forgiveness for that foe.
There is transformation for that turmoil.
There is love in your life.

I have a dream that Jesus has overcome this world (John 16:33[18]) and there is a place for us losers.

When I was in 6th grade, I wrote this prayer for my confirmation class (the prayer that led to me winning the "Grand Prize" for "Why I Want to be a Christian.")

This was my prayer:

"Dear Lord, please 'o' please let all this violence stop in the world. Let this be a peaceful world where everybody is 'cool.' Let me and all the other unsuccessful boys who are considered wimps, girls, tattletales, smarty pants, and nerds all have a time where we are famous, strong, and not only having a good time at church but everywhere. Please help me make the right decisions in life. I love you, Lord, (and) I believe in you. In your name we pray, Amen."
  -   Russell Clark, 6th grade[19]

There is a place where we are no longer left out. There is a place for losers like you and me

Chapter 2:
The Dying Church & The Spiky-haired Pastor

"Russell! What. The. Hell. Are. You. DOING?!"

I'm a little drunk. Oh, that's my wife yelling at me. I'm only trying to go to the bathroom. In the trash can. In the kitchen. At my father-in-law's house. My bad.

The day was July 4, 2013. I woke up drinking beer that day and continued until after the fireworks went off. That's because I was attempting to erase the conversation I had the day before when I realized my career as a pastor was over.

//

A month earlier I had been at Annual Conference – the yearly gathering of United Methodists – and I was trying to reintroduce myself to the pastors in Texas. I had just spent three years in Florida having the time of my life at a small-town church in Reddick, Florida. Now, back in my home state, most people just shrugged me off as the spiky-haired kid who stood up to The Bitch. Some of them flat out ignored me as I tried to reconnect with them. I'm just that immature turd who doesn't respect authority and most church leaders wouldn't even make eye contact with me because they knew what was about to happen to me. I had already been told they didn't have a pastoral appointment for me but little did I know what was about to go down.

I was feeling really lonely until I ran into a friend of mine, Alan, who yanked me upstairs because he wanted to introduce me to someone.

"Joe is as goofy as you. He has a similar story to yours. He started a new church and he hates rules as much as you do."

In a crowd of men in suits and ties and women in nice dresses, Joe was wearing a brightly colored Hawaiian shirt. As I was introduced to him, one of the other pastors yelled out sarcastically, "Hey Joe! Thanks so much for dressing up for the occasion!"

"This is my Sunday best," he bantered back.

This shining, smiling, dynamic character, Joe, took me out to lunch. As we scarfed down chips & salsa, he insisted on hearing my story. I told him about my time serving in Reddick and how we were featured on the front page of the United Methodist Church webpage for having the "secret to church growth." [20] And how these last few years have been about reaching out to young people but also making sure we didn't forget about our old, seasoned members as every generation learned how to work together and be the church together. I mentioned that my return back home to Texas hadn't exactly been like the prodigal son returning home. Instead of a party, I was told there wasn't an appointment for me.

Joe and I immediately clicked and he later told me he wanted to bring me on his church staff, in hopes of me possibly taking over his church when he planned to retire the following year.

I mentioned that out of respect we should tell the district superintendent he was going to hire me.

Then I received a phone call on July 3, 2013.

"Russell, I told you I would be honest with you about my conversation with the district superintendent. He told me not to hire you. I was told to not be 'confused by your resume.' That hiring you would be a *mistake*."

Not only was I not going to have an appointment as a pastor but now I was not even able to get a *job* at a church in Texas without being blackballed.

Totally and utterly deflated.

I wanted to cry. And I did. I wanted to throw things. And I did. I practically swam in a pool of alcohol the next day trying to erase pain of having the last 10 years – where I had poured my heart and soul into ministry – ripped away.

//

After peeing in the trash can at my father-in-law's house, it took me a month to get a meeting with the district superintendent. The conference was not going to welcome me back. I was told the church growth I had in Florida was only temporary. The district superintendent said if I had stayed there longer the church would have realized it's really "all about me." He said the truth is I don't respect authority and don't understand emotional context. He was right because I was full of emotions at that very moment and I didn't hide them very well. I've never been afraid to be vulnerable and share the full truth about who I am and what I've experienced.

"Would you like me to set up a visit with a career counselor?"

I snapped. A career counselor?! What is happening?!

"I'm a pastor! All I've ever wanted to do since high school was be in ministry! And I'm a *great* pastor! I know I am!"

But it's funny that what this man said about me – who I had never met before – were the same things The Bitch used to say about me word-for-word.

"Sir, you've never met me before," I said as I was holding back tears and frustration. "And I wish I could have told you my story. But you've already been told who I am by someone else. I wish you could have gotten to know my true self, who God made me to be. Not what this woman told you I am."

Like the saying goes "insanity is doing the same thing over and over again and expecting different results."

As I walked out of his office, I left the United Methodist Church forever and I've never looked back.

//

Three years *prior* to that fateful meeting, a woman with her back hunched over was using a walker to slowly walk down the church aisle, making her way to speak to me after worship.

Ms. Eva – a 93-years young, seasoned woman – was sure to tell me how she felt about me – a 29-year old, spiky-haired, energetic kid – being her pastor.

"Well, that was the first time I heard a pastor use different accents."
"Well, that was the first time I could actually hear the pastor the whole time."
"Well, I've never seen a pastor use funny hats before."
"Well, I've never seen a pastor with hair that tall."
"Are you growing a beard as a disguise from the cops or something?"

Every time I saw Ms. Eva I'd ask her how she was doing and her response was always, *"I'm mean!"*

Other than our sense of humor, you wouldn't exactly think this spiky-haired kid would be her choice of pastor but one Sunday she pulled me aside:

"Russell, you're the best pastor we've ever had."

After moving to Florida, I had been humbled. My bad experience with The Bitch caused me to almost leave ministry altogether. I was a nobody from Texas just hoping I could get an appointment at a church, any church.

Like the young David in the bible, I felt dismissed by my brothers and father but still anointed by God and ready to face my Goliath. [21] Before I left Texas to move to Florida, the board of ordained ministry told me I had "bad grammar" and that's why I would have to come back to see them next year to try to continue on the process towards ordination. I didn't know my calling couldn't have sentence fragments and run-on sentences.

So, I brushed off my feet and cut ties with Texas to start a new life in Florida. Before The Bitch and the cabinet destroyed me three years later, my life as a pastor would get its one and only shot in the smallest town I've ever seen.

Before the district superintendent in Florida appointed me to Reddick United Methodist Church, she told me "most people don't want to work at a church like this."

But I was in no position to be picky.

//

John 4 talks about Jesus sitting down with a Samaritan woman at the well. [22] This was a problem because Jesus was a Jew, a man, and not this woman's husband. But he sat down with this Samaritan woman ignoring all the rules.

He asked her for some water.

"Who are you to ask me for some water?"

Translation: "Oh no you didn't!" (diva finger snap)

Jesus told her she should be less concerned about the water he's asking for and more concerned with the everlasting water of life he has.

I'm sure she was about ready to pull out her pepper spray but she hesitantly listened.

He casually mentioned her husband in their conversation.

"Ha ha. I don't have a husband."

"Well, in fact, you have five husbands and the man you're sleeping with now is not even your husband."

Who is this man who knows everything about me?

Jesus mentioned worship and she was quick to tell him that Jews worshipped in their temple and she worshiped here in Samaria.

Jesus told her there is a time when what you're called and where you worship will not matter. True worship is from your heart.

"It's who you are and the way you live that count before God. Your worship must engage your spirit in the pursuit of truth. That's the kind of people the Father is out looking for: those who are simply and honestly themselves before him in their worship. God is sheer being itself – Spirit. Those who worship him must do it out of their very being, their spirits, their true selves, in adoration." [23]

Simple. Honest. True.

That's what matters. That's what The Father is after.

Jesus showed this woman he sees her and loves her in their short conversation. And that God is after raw, authentic devotion.

This short conversation rocked her world. At the core, this woman was shown she is *known* and *loved* for exactly who she is. He told her to pursue what really matters.

True worship.

//

Growing up watching old, white men preach I was bored to death. I would make fun of the pastors with my family, especially when they did the same sermon at Christmas two years in a row. I suppose this is where my lack of respect for authority started.

Sitting in the church pew listening to the pale-skinned preacher talk about God I thought,

"Why is he making God sound so boring?"

God is not boring!

God is exciting! God is real, in-your-face, sitting down with you at the well even though he's not supposed to. He's telling you secrets about your life and about what life should really be about.

Jesus might be odd and crazy, maybe. But certainly anything but boring!

He talks about this everlasting water, which he says flows freely forever. Think you're thirsty? He says you'll never thirst again with the water he offers. This water never stops.

This water is a metaphor for receiving that spiritual nourishment we need.

Jesus is God in heaven sitting down with us on earth showing us that worship is right here, right now. God's presence is with you at the coffee shop, the grocery store, the liquor store, the soccer field, as you climb that career ladder, as you sit at home "Netflix and chilling."

He's showing you that wherever you are there's more going on than you realize. He sees you, knows you, and loves you.

He broke the God rule and became one of us. He continued breaking the rules to always be with us. He died and broke that stay-dead rule. He comes into your heart and transforms your life in ways you never knew possible.

I know this is true because from the time I sat in church knowing God is not boring, from being on mission trips and going through confirmation in 6th grade, even that night I was drunk peeing in a trash can….

God has transformed my life. He has sat with me in my mess. He's listened to my junk and the bull I've tried to tell him was true. He's told me what story is *actually* true about my life and how I should think and live.

He told me what true worship looks like. He's shown me who he is and even though he knows all my junk, he still sits with me and loves me.

When I was in college, I remember walking out of my job as a waiter because I wanted to do something more meaningful. I wanted the world to know God is not boring. It was shortly after being on a mission trip that I realized my calling was more than asking patrons what type of alcoholic beverage they prefer.

I worked at a pharmacy for years when I was making $300 a month starting out as a youth minister and had to work a second job to make ends meet. It was a challenge dealing with customers who were either mad at their doctor, the pharmacist for taking too long, their insurance for raising the cost of the prescription, or their illness for kicking their butt. This was great preparation for dealing with cranky, sick people in the church.

I was willing to work two jobs and make nothing as a youth minister because this is what I loved to do. I wanted others to know the exciting God I came to know and love, the God I found because he first loved me.

Being a pastor was never about the power. I continually forgot about the ordination paperwork to become a "real" pastor because I was more focused on sitting with teenagers listening to their problems and making them feel known and loved.

When I was a youth minister, the youth and church members made me a pastoral stole with their handprints and signatures on it. Pastors are not supposed to wear stoles until they are ordained. But they said "you might not be ordained yet but we already see you as Reverend."

The first time the kids at my new church in Florida called me "Pastor Russell," I knew I had arrived.

//

Because I wasn't ordained yet and wasn't a part of the Florida Annual Conference yet, I had to have another pastor "bless the elements" for communion for me.

I met with this pastor for lunch at Chili's and then afterwards we went to my car where I had the bread and juice for him to bless for me. A car drove by blasting Twisted Sister's "We're Not Gonna Take It" as he prayed over the elements for communion.

"Twisted Sister is perfect music for blessing the elements," he said as we both laughed.

I mentioned this exchange to two of the church leaders at my new church.

"I hate these stupid rules! Why do I have to bless these elements in a restaurant parking lot when it's God who gives me the authority to be your pastor?! Not the church leaders who haven't transferred me to the Florida conference yet! And not this pastor who blessed these elements! But it's God's power working through me and this bread and juice that gives it meaning! That's what's real."

"Russell, we totally agree. It's stupid. We're okay with you blessing the elements yourself and never doing that again. We hate the church's stupid rules too. These church leaders need to stop telling us what to do and let us be our own church."

This dying church in Florida was a place many pastors didn't want to work because it was full of stubborn, seasoned members. I was a spiky-haired loser from Texas who was about to be kicked out of the church upon my return to Texas.

But like Jesus sitting down with the Samaritan woman and breaking all the rules, this church and I were the odd couple who was able to love each other when we both needed it the most.

At this time,
In this moment,
In Reddick, Florida,

This dying church and spiky-haired pastor were prepared to break all the rules.

And we just so happened to be the perfect fit.

Chapter 3:
2 Chairs

"The church leaders asked me if it was too much to expect their pastor to be at their monthly Wednesday night dinner," my Florida District Superintendent explained.

The previous pastor at the church in Reddick before me showed up to deliver a sermon on Sunday mornings and the members of the church never saw her the rest of the week. And she lived in the parsonage next to the church.

"These church members are simply looking for someone to give them their time and attention."

Before my first Sunday in Reddick, I went to visit one of their members, Susan, who was terminally ill with cancer. She was receiving hospice care in her home. She was wearing a faded nightgown and she had a breathing tube in her nose connected to an oxygen tank. They had moved her bed out into the living room next to the window where she had a view of their large front yard. This was one of my first experiences with someone who had cancer.

"You're the new pastor? I'm pretty sure I have shoes older than you! That's so wonderful. And thank you for coming here. The other pastor never came to see me once."

She began talking to me like we had known each other for years. She told me stories about her family and the church. She said she did not get up in front of the church to talk to people so don't even ask her. I said that's perfectly okay and I wouldn't. We both laughed.

You could feel how hard it was for her to move. But in the midst of this weakness you could also sense a great strength. The way she talked about her faith while dealing with cancer was like watching her weak, sick body lift a semi-truck. I had met Wonder Woman in the flesh.

She pulled out a small pillow from the side of her bed that said "Hope." She told me this tiny bag filled with cotton – and the word stitched on the front of it – changed her life because it represented the God who had power over her cancer and death itself. I couldn't help but think about how Superman's "S" on his chest also meant hope.

She showed me blankets she had made which she had in bed with her.

"I've made blankets for just about every baby that's been born in our little church. I know that isn't much…."

"Oh, yes, it is!" I interrupted her. "I'm sure that's a big help for new families. And it makes them feel loved and cared for."

She looked me straight in the eye and told me she was not done yet here on this earth.

"I know I am supposed to help more people. I am here because I'm not done helping people. I don't know what it is I'm supposed to do, but I am going to help more people. I'm not done yet. Russell, don't get me wrong, I'm not afraid to die. I just know I'm not done yet. But when I meet God I hope he tells me I helped to shine the light of Christ for other people."

She then stopped herself and started to cry a little.

Then, I grabbed her hand and told her what I had planned for children's time for my first Sunday. In the Pixar film *Up*,[24] there is a dog, Dug. Dug has a voice box his master made for him that helps him to talk like humans. So, whenever Dug meets someone he says, "Hi, my name is

Dug. I just met you and I love you." My plan for my first Sunday was to tell the kids and adults that I just met them and I already loved them.

Holding Susan's hand, I looked her in the eye and said, "Susan, I know that I just met you but I feel like I have known you for years. You have touched my life greatly in this last hour we've been talking. I love you already.

She said, "I love you too. I can tell that God has brought you here to our church for a reason. I know God is going to do great things for our church through you."

//

Emmitt Smith has always been one of my favorite football players. I grew up in Arlington, Texas and I've always been a big fan of the Dallas Cowboys.

One evening I was watching Emmitt Smith's induction into the hall of fame. I'll never forget one statement he made in his speech:

"A dream is only a dream if you never write it down. Once you write down your dream, it becomes a goal."[25]

At my first leadership retreat as the new senior pastor at First United Methodist Church in Reddick, Florida, I told them about Emmitt's statement.

Like I said, when I first came to Reddick, it was the smallest church in the smallest town I've ever seen. There is one stop sign as you pass through Reddick. There isn't even a stop light. This was a major culture shock from the big city I came from, although I was thankful not to have to worry about any red light cameras anymore. My bank account still thanks you, Reddick.

At this leadership retreat, I said to the church leaders:

"I don't care about us making goals that we're never serious about accomplishing. I don't want us to dream up goals that are impossible for us to accomplish just so we can say we came up with ideas at this leadership retreat. I want us to believe that if we write these goals down we *can* accomplish them. We need to make practical goals that, when we write them down, we know we're *going* to make this happen."

I also made an important statement that day – something I felt truly passionate about at the time:

"And I don't care if we get more money in this church or if we get more church members. Changing our statistics so we look good shouldn't be our main goal or priority. What I care about is that we are *growing spiritually*. If we are doing that, these others areas will take care of themselves."

After 2 ½ years serving in Reddick since then, we transformed from 15 persons in worship to 115. We went from a church which couldn't pay its bills to a church which was self-sufficient and able to do unbelievable ministry for persons in need and our youth. Any District Superintendent of the United Methodist Church would love to hear that we also had paid 100% of our apportionments (Apportionments are the tithe United Methodist pay to the conference to help various needs).

//

The church leaders insisted I wear a minister's robe to worship on my first Sunday. In July. In Florida. I was sweating bullets by the time the service was over. But I did it anyway to respect them and showed I cared about what they wanted.

They also insisted that I have set office hours so I'd be readily available for church members to stop by and visit.

After only a month, they didn't care about the robe or the office hours anymore. They already knew that I loved and cared for them and that I'd be around often to visit with.

"The kids are coming back to church!" was the common phrase I heard. This meant that adults under 50 were coming back to church.

This church never had a large budget. We never had marketing tools or an evangelism strategy. We couldn't afford billboards or a church marquee to advertise what we were doing or mailers to send out to the community. What we had were church leaders who believed they could dream up bigger goals than they had done before. We started becoming excited for the church we believed we could become. We grew simply by word-of-mouth because people were telling their friends, family members, co-workers, neighbors, and random people at the grocery story that we were a church that did things a little differently. It was all word-of-mouth *excitement* that led the "kids" to come back to church.

When actual kids and teenagers started to attend the church, other pastors in the area caught word of it.

"How are you getting young people to *want* to come to church?"

"We spend time with them. It's that simple. We have fun in church. We've had overnight lock-ins, we had an ice cream slip 'n' slide, and we had a 'Sunrise to Sunset' trip where we went from the east coast of Florida to watch the sunrise then drove to the west coast to watch the sunset that evening.

"We sing songs they enjoy. The church leaders actually told *me* they want to bring in contemporary music for the young people and I was hesitant about how others would react. They said, 'But Russell, *we got used to you. Certainly we can get used to contemporary music.*'"

I was told I had some balls introducing a projector and contemporary music in that old, country church. But for the few that had resistance towards it they looked around and saw all the young people, the new faces standing beside them – and suddenly it didn't matter anymore.

When I first started telling jokes in my sermons, they didn't know if it was okay to laugh in church but soon we all belly-laughed together.

We celebrated our accomplishments together. One Sunday we had 26 new members join the church! *Twenty-six!*

One of them was the pianist's husband who spent every prior Sunday at the golf course and then he started coming to church! He joined the church…along with his brother!

Another was a family who came to church because of my "Superheroes and Scripture" sermon series. Since I've left, he is now the chair of the Staff/Parish Relations Committee and they're big leaders in the church themselves!

Another family had "rebellious" teenagers they were raising. They first came to church at an overnight lock-in and one of the adults didn't care much for their loud, disrespectful attitude. But the next morning their mom told me that was the first time she had been able to get her kids out of the house in a long time… and this was to have fun at church! She and her husband and three boys came to church practically every Sunday after that!

After 26 members joined one Sunday, I just sat in awe of God afterwards thinking this is something this church will always talk about. They will always remember this. God had certainly turned around this dying church (and that loser who became their spiky-haired pastor).

One of our older members told me that my sermons were great because she could see the children and youth paying attention. She knew they would ask their mom questions about the sermon showing they were listening.

I leaned in and whispered to my old, retired friend and said, "But don't older people deserve a sermon that doesn't put them to sleep also? Not that I'm saying you're old, of course."

Another church member – a vice principal at the middle school – told me her co-workers asked if she had been seeing a counselor because she was in a much better mood. Her response: "No, my pastor's sermons have just been really great lately."

But what I was doing wasn't anything special. I felt like we were simply doing what the other pastor should have been doing in the first place. I gave them my time. I ate donuts and talked about Gator football with the retired people. I sang camp songs and played tag with the kids.

I showed them that *God is not boring*. God is ever-present in every aspect of our lives.

One church member referred to it this way:

"I just wanted to say thank you for breathing some life into our church. My wife and I have not seen it filled with this kind of energy in *years*."

My calling was alive and flourishing.

//

One weekend my wife & I were invited to hang out with a group of adults from the church. I asked my wife, Shannon, if I should bring beer or not.

"I don't want to make them uncomfortable by not drinking beer, but I don't want to make it weird by me bringing beer either."

When I walked in the door to their home, all the men stared at me as I set down my tiny cooler and pulled out a beer. As I popped the tab, they all breathed out a huge sigh of relief.

"Woo! We're so glad you brought beer! We would have never invited you back if you didn't!"

Those men became some of my best friends throughout the next few years. And they still are to this day.

//

One Sunday I asked the church what it would look like if we took everything out of the church.

The pews, the piano, the organ, the altar, the communion table, the cross, the bible, the picture of Jesus (that I was told my first Sunday shall never come down).

If we were left with a blank, empty space in the church, what should we add back to make the church *really* be a church?

Normal answers were shouted out like, "Jesus!", "God!", "The Cross!", "The bible!"

Then one smart ass said, "A chair!"

A chair.

The first thing we would need to add back to the church to make it a church would be a chair.

"You're right."

A place to sit. But it's more than that. It's a place for you.

A chair *for you*.

To show this church is your home. You belong here.

God's story is your story. This church's story is your story.

You're part of this family.

You belong.

There is a chair waiting for you.

The 2nd thing we need to make a church *really* be a church is… what?

"Another chair."

We need someone to sit with.

Someone who will give us time and attention.
Someone who will sit with us and cry with us when we find out we have cancer.
Someone who will laugh with us and play duck, duck goose with us.
Someone who will talk about football and drink beer with us.
Someone who won't care about the money we give or if we go to the golf course one Sunday but will deeply care about our lives and will love us like family.

Because that's the kind of love Jesus first showed to us.

If we're going to make a church look like God's holy, sacred place, then a good place to start is with 2 chairs.

There's a place for you.
And there's someone to sit with you.
That's church.

Chapter 4:
OWESOME

OWESOME (pronounced ow • sum) = the ultimate epitomization of being awesome; the confidence one finds from living an exciting, passionate new life in Jesus Christ; awareness and/or discovery of the love & grace of God in everyday life; living to humbly love & serve all people; ex. *"God made you to be OWESOME!", "That mission trip was OWESOME!"*

//

One of the first lessons I was taught as a pastor in Reddick is you don't ever plan a church event during a Florida Gators football game. Gator football is as sacred to them as the ancient Jesus picture they have behind the altar (which I'm certain will be hung up as long as Reddick United Methodist Church is still rocking).

Another lesson I quickly learned from the good people in Reddick being close to Gator Nation (The University of Florida in Gainesville) is you don't talk bad about Tebow.

Tim Tebow – The Heisman winning quarterback who played for the Gators and had a short but highly publicized career in the NFL – is the subject of much criticism. ESPN analysts said he would never make it as an NFL quarterback. When he decided to play baseball, they were quick to shut down those dreams too. Even preachers have said he's a hypocrite for praying in front of millions of people during the "Tebowing" craze.

But people didn't talk about his talent to play sports as much as they did his faith.

Before the "Tebowing" phenomenon of 2011, my church members talked me into reading *Through My Eyes* by Tim Tebow.[26]

Tebow's commitment to use his fame and wealth for good is admirable. What amazes me the most about Tebow is his passion – his commitment to drive himself to be the best at everything he does. He has a passion for God and compassion for people that is undeniable. He didn't ask for "Tebowing" to become a trend. He wasn't asking for the cameras to be on him every time he prayed. His parents just taught him that when you need to pray, pray. Tebowing should have been a simple statement of Tebow's authentic character; not some sort of need for attention.

Tebow has this drive to push himself unlike anyone I've ever seen. His workout plan is insane! When critics said he'll never make it in the NFL, I know that was only inspiration for him to work harder. He might have been a loser who never made it in the NFL and he may never make it in baseball either but you can't knock the man for ignoring critics and following his dreams.

Criticism can inspire change.

If you're doing something meaningful, critics will show up out of the woodworks. If you're doing something which sets you apart from the crowd, people will pay attention.

Jesus says in John 16:33 that in this world we will have trouble.[27] No doubt about it.

I was certainly inspired in Reddick by all the ways we were told the church *can't* change or what I *can't* do. It's easy to talk about the trouble we face as Christians. As David Kinnaman says, "Christianity has an image problem."[28] With all the pastors I've worked with, I've learned just as much from them about what type of pastor I *want* to be as I have the type of pastor I *never* want to be.

"In this world you will have trouble. But take heart! I have overcome the world." – Jesus in John 16:33[29]

Netflix made a popular show about a teen committing suicide, *13 Reasons Why*.[30] This show bugged me because it romanticized suicide without showing sufficient redemption. How could this have been avoided? How could we tell a different story about 13 reasons why *not* to commit suicide? A common phrase used in the show was, "F*** my life." I wanted to hear about why we should "*Love* my life."

The story I wanted to hear is about how, by God's grace, we can overcome it. Things get better. We can be who God has called each of us to be. We can be different than the world around us. We can be different than the *churches* around us. We can fight off the critics and be our true selves, who God has made us to be.

I have a bookmark that says, "Hold an image of the life you want…and that dream will become a reality."

I believe in a Church that can be what God originally intended for it to be. No longer will people say like Gandhi, "I like your Christ, I do not like your Christians. Your Christians are so unlike your Christ."[31] We can stop the world (and pastors) from continually saying how we've got it *wrong*…

…And show the world how we've got it *right*.

I don't know if Tebow was depressed that he never became a Superbowl champion. Tebow *is* a Heisman winner. No one can take that accomplishment away from him. Even more than that, he is a man of faith who has touched many with his philanthropic work.

I just have a hunch that whatever Tebow's goals are the goals are not what inspire him the most. I don't think the end goal is what drives him. It's the drive itself. It's the journey. I think his drive to be *more* comes from his faith in who God says he is.

Fan or critic, I think Tebow's relentless passion for faith and football (and now baseball) are undeniable.

Even though Tebow is no longer playing for the NFL and he might never make it to the MLB, no one can deny the impact he has had on sports and its fans. He has used the platform he has been given to make an even greater impact through the Tim Tebow Foundation and his orphanage in the Philippines.

Tebow believes God made him to be OWESOME!

//

My senior year in high school I wanted to do the testimony on Youth Sunday. So I signed up. I believed I could say something worthwhile, and that I could say it in a way that would mean something to the congregation and my friends. I don't remember how, but God just gave me the words to say. I wrote out my message because I wanted to be sure the message was clear and succinct. This was the first sermon I ever gave in my life.

I talked about my friend, O.J., who had committed suicide. He was going into 9th grade. His suicide brought our youth group closer together after experiencing such heartache. We had to rely on each other for strength because that situation was harder to understand than anything any of us had experienced. I was thankful for how close our youth group was after that, but I asked the question, *"Why does it take someone losing their life for us to realize how much we need Jesus and each other?"*

I talked about how we had 46 confirmation students when I was in 6th grade and now by my senior year, just 6 of the 46 students were still active in our church. My parents used to make me come to church – and not just make me – *drag* me kicking and screaming. I would fight them all the way there. I would whine and complain about how I just didn't want to go, but once I got there I always had fun.

Now, in my senior year, my youth group meant so much to me that I wouldn't dream of being anywhere else. I came to church even when my parents didn't. I begged and pleaded for my boss at my job not to schedule me on Sundays so I could remain active in the youth group. I found God through my friends in my youth group.

When I attended a youth minister training camp, every person there said they wanted to be a youth minister because their youth group was horrible or their youth minister was horrible. I was the only one who said, "Well, the reason I want to be a youth minister is because my youth group meant so much to me and my youth minister helped me out so much that I want everyone to have the same experience I have had. I want everyone to experience the love that I have experienced."

I remember being in 7th grade and wanting to be like all of the Senior High kids in my youth group. We went to a place called Burger's Lake with all of them. When these Senior High kids talked to a little minion like me I was over the moon. Having been bullied at this age, I didn't have much self-worth.

But when I came to church I wasn't a loser.

I was cool.
I was accepted.
I was loved.

In 9th grade, I almost gave up on going to church. I wasn't sure I connected with anyone at church anymore. It all began to feel pointless.

Then I went on my first mission trip. I felt connected with friends at church more than ever. I had more fun than I had ever had before. My eyes were opened to see how lucky I was because I saw the conditions of the clients we served.

After my first mission trip, my passion for church was unquenchable. I could have had the worst week in my dramatic teenage life, but then I stepped into the youth building with the multi-colored chairs and played foosball with my church friends and my whole world felt complete again.

I had a special bond with four people: Aaron, David, Stephanie, and Robyn. The five of us together were inseparable.

When we were in high school, we would stay after youth meetings talking and laughing in the parking lot for hours. We were always focused on growing with God, enjoying each other's presence, and helping each other out. Back then, though, I didn't know how meaningful our relationships were shaping me to be who I am. All I would have said about our friendships back then was that we had "something special."

These friends at church were my true friends and we loved each other exactly the way we were. I knew they were my true friends because whenever we fought over something, we always apologized to each other. Whenever anyone was in a bad mood, we were always there to talk, to cry, to stand up, and move forward together.

We watched our crazy youth minister and other adult leaders act like bigger kids than we ever did. They were pulling pranks, telling stupid jokes, and making fools out of themselves like the rest of us. They showed us Christ by first letting loose and acting like God's children. Then they showed us they truly, deeply cared for us as they helped guide us to the path we were called to be on.

I can look back on my life now and see how these relationships were beyond value. The love I share today is because of the love they first shared with me. I found out who I am and who I am called to be through these adults and students who were truly God's presence for me.

I never felt like God spoke to me when I was young, but I could always hear God talking to me through my friends. I learned to always open myself up with them and share my deepest pains and secrets because I knew I could trust them. They would listen, pray for me, and help me refocus on who God made me to be.

Each friend had a different gift. Aaron would keep me humble and help me watch my pride. And he was the one to encourage me to stand up for myself. David was the bible nerd who could help us find that biblical perspective to life. Stephanie was full of joy and could always put a smile on our faces. Robyn was the embodiment of love, and as she cared for us, we knew how to care for others.

After I gave that testimony on Youth Sunday, one of the moms came up to me and the pastor and said, "You need to get this kid started in ministry." And then when I continued to give devotionals on the ski trips and mission trips, every time I received hugs and letters affirming that this was what I was supposed to do. I started questioning what I was called to do and realized I had a gift of talking to people that I needed to share.

But this calling didn't start here. It didn't happen because I started wondering what I wanted to do with my life. My calling to be something completely wild happened when these wild people decided to share this wild and crazy love with me – not just by their words, but their actions.

I am who I am today because I found true friends in the body of Christ.

//

Years ago I followed the singer, Marilyn Manson. He called himself the antichrist. His music was very angry and demented, but there was something deeper than his anger.

He was hurt. He was in pain.

I heard a story long ago that when he was at his church as a teenager, he didn't have the same joyful experience as I did growing up in church. His youth group was not accepting or loving because he was different. He felt unwanted like an outcast in the one place where outcasts are supposed to be welcome.

It's no wonder he calls himself the antichrist. Because the people who were supposed to be God's presence for him instead were the opposite. They robbed him of experiencing God's love.

Why give God the time of day if God's people made you feel like more of a loser?

At Burger's Lake, where the Senior High made me feel special and began this process of molding my life into something OWESOME, there was another boy in 7th grade.

I watched him get made fun of by the same people that made me feel cool. I remember watching him getting made fun of and wishing my puny, 7th grade, loser self would have say something, do something. But what could I have done when I was struggling to be accepted and loved myself?

This boy left the church. His family still showed up, but he refused to come with them. When he did come to church, he stayed in a corner, talked to no one, and was often so excluded he was practically invisible to the rest of us.

Today he has a beautiful son and wife and from what I can see he has a beautiful life. But I believe he is still an atheist.

His teenage years could have been much different if Senior High boys didn't make him feel worthless in 7th grade.

//

When I was robbed of my career as a minister, my memories of feeling loved and accepted – which once brought me joy – were suddenly filled with pain. I questioned if this love I experienced all my life was ever real.

I felt more like I was actually the other boy being rejected.
I wasn't the prodigal son being welcomed home with a party.
I was the kid being unwillingly dunked in the lake by my peers.
My comforting home I had known since childhood burned to the ground.

And I found myself questioning everything.

If you've seen the Pixar film *Inside Out*, it is about the voices inside our heads and our memories. The voice, Joy, has created many happy memories for her girl, Riley. But when Riley is forced to move away from her friends to a new town these happy memories are touched by another voice, Sadness. Sadness turns these once shining memories blue.[32]

That's what happens when someone betrays us. That's what it looks like when someone rips out our heart and all the joy and love we once experienced is tainted. These once bright, yellow memories turn blue.

And sometimes those joyful memories never come back. And they will never look the same ever again.

Like that other little boy, I knew what it felt like for the church to do the opposite of what it is supposed to do.

Like Marilyn Manson, I felt that deep hurt and pain that makes one want to sing and scream with anger of how the church robbed us of love.

It's true we each have a free will to choose whether to follow God or not, but we can sure *help* or *hinder* someone from finding out they can find the life of love they are looking for in Jesus Christ. You and I know there is something wrong with the Church today because many people feel more hurt from what is happening in churches than help.

Instead of loving people for who they are, churches are condemning people to hell for who they are. They might even preach the love of Christ but their actions produce the antichrist.

Our actions and love for each other speak much more than any eloquent words we could ever say.

Who cares if your church marquee speaks of love if the people in the pews ignore the broken, the outcast, the disheartened who need a good word now more than ever?

//

The church or church leaders or Christians may have robbed you of joy for a time but I'm here to tell you God's love is still real.

This unconditional love is real. It's OWESOME!

My friend, Tom, said, "*Russell, you always preached about being a minister for the outcasts and losers and helping them see they are made to be OWESOME. Now, you know what it feels like to be an outcast too.*

You know what it feels like to have the church do the opposite of what they're supposed to."

Jesus says in Luke 9:24, *"Those who try to save their lives will lose it, but those who lose their lives for my sake will find it."*[33]

For those of you who have lost careers, you still have purpose for a new day.
For those of you who have lost relationships, you are still worthy of love.
For those of you who have lost your innocence when you did something unimaginable, or had something unimaginable happen to you, there is healing and renewal so you can move forward.
For those of you who have lost someone close to you, there is life beyond grief.
For those of you who have lost your faith, there is still hope to find it again.
For those of you who have lost who you are, you can still reclaim your true self, who you are meant to be.

It's time to let you know one thing.

You.
Are.
Still.
Worth.
It.

To God. To me. To God's people.

You are worth it.

The church might have betrayed you and condemned you to hell.
The person who was supposed to love you might have abused you and left you.
The joyful memories you once had might have been shattered and feel like they'll never return.
Depression could be eating you alive because life doesn't look like what you thought it would.
The church hasn't been what it should.

Your family and friends might not accept you and love you for who you are.

But you are worth it.

God thinks of you and smiles. God rejoices at the thought of you.

I know it.

God made you to be OWESOME!

And I'm not talking about awesome like you've heard it said, like nerdy "awesome". I am talking about OWESOME!

It's a raw, real, gritty, passionate way of saying awesome.

OWESOME!

As Rob Bell says, "The church is not a building. Church is people. People whose hearts are beating more and more like God's."[34]

The church is the *people!*

The church doesn't exist without two chairs: a chair for you and someone to sit with you! We've forgotten the simplicity of loving one another and being there for one another! We've forgotten the need to simply make "room at the inn" for someone in need!

Everything we do – from taking care of our families, to going to school and work, to hanging out with friends, from changing the way we think about ourselves, to loving people right where they are, from starting a revolution of God's love here & now in our everyday lives, from the children to the youth to the adults…

Everything is centered around the love we have for God and the love we have for each other!

That's it.

That's church, people.

And it's not a building.

It is hearts centered on two things:

Love God.
Love others.

If we have forgotten about love, we have forgotten what it looks like to be OWESOME, to be who God made us to be.

Love is our only reality.
And this love is forever.
And this love is OWESOME.

And this love puts us in check because we realize we can't live up to this unconditional love. We've fallen short of loving people where they are. We haven't helped the church be what it was supposed to be all the time. We're a little – no, we're all sorts of messed up. And that's why we all need grace.

Grace is such an important word. Grace is the love from God that is undeserved and unmerited. It is without condition.

It is this love that loves our messed up, rotten, dirty, disgusting selves and says, "I love you simply because you are God's child."

God says, "I will always love you because you are my child."

We can't earn God's love. That's why it's called *grace*. There is nothing we can do to be worthy of this love. God loves us while we're still sinners. God loves us right where we are, and this is why we can love others right where they are.

Love people right where they are.

That's one of the most important lessons we can ever learn.

Love people right where they are.

Love.

This word – love – wouldn't mean anything to me if I didn't see the love of Christ growing up.

Before I was able to grasp how I should think about God, how I should know and come to understand what the Gospel – the good news – was all about. Before I knew the story of Jesus' life, death, and resurrection.

Before I knew this Gospel story, before I could understand all of this…. And before the church robbed me of joy for a time…

I *saw* the love of Christ.

I saw who I was supposed to be by the love people *like you* have shown me.

I found the confidence to be somebody because of God's presence working through OWESOME losers like you.

We say, "I am young. Who am I? I don't have any money. I don't have a car. I'm not that smart. I'm a nerd. I'm a loser."

"You are God's child! God made you to be OWESOME!"

We say, "I am old. Who am I? I can barely walk. I am sick and tired. I don't have any energy like these young whipper-snappers."

"You are God's child! God has a purpose for you today! God made you to be OWESOME!"

We say, "I am gay. I am a woman. I am a person of color. I am nothing to society…"

//

I have been to Ebenezer Baptist Church in Atlanta, Georgia a couple times. You can just feel the power standing in Martin Luther King, Jr's church. This was the place history was made. This was the place a revolution was born.

I was in this old church looking at pictures of Dr. King preaching in the very room I was standing. I was looking out at the pews and looking back at the congregation in the picture. I stood in the sanctuary and admired Dr. King's pulpit.

"This church doesn't look much different than the one I've been preaching in. This city church isn't much bigger than our old, country church. It doesn't look much different than Mt. Zion United Methodist Church, the African American church down the street. This church has about as many people as we have on a good Sunday. It wasn't thousands of people. It was maybe a hundred people, if that."

And those people made history. Those people started a revolution. Those people were inspired by the confidence of the Holy Spirit to be OWESOME!

We might say of ourselves, "I am a person of color. I am a person of injustice and persecution. I am gay. I am a woman. I am nothing to my church or society."

"You are God's child! God made you to be OWESOME!"

No matter what color you are, no matter what clothes you wear, no matter how intelligent or unintelligent you are, no matter your sexual preference, no matter your gender, no matter your political preference, no matter if you're single, married, divorced, or remarried, no matter your appearance, no matter how you smell, no matter how you talk or don't talk, no matter what your Facebook page looks like, no matter how many followers you have on Instagram, no matter how good you are, no matter how cool you are, no matter how young or old you are…

May you shatter your insecurities and the injustices around you and within you to have the courageous confidence in the Holy Spirit that God made you to be OWESOME!

Remember: God became *nothing* and became a servant – a *loser* – and lost his life on the cross only to be raised up so we could know…

Death is not the end.

Our insecurities don't have the final word.
Our sin and shame don't destroy us.
These corrupt authorities and bullies don't rule over us.
These injustices don't compare to the long walk of justice we are on.

Through God in Jesus in the Holy Spirit, we also can see that living the way God calls us to live is the only way to live freely.

We are called to be wild losers!
We are called to be OWESOME!

OWESOME in a way that's different than anything we've ever experienced before!
OWESOME where we know we have lost our lives only to find it to be transformed!
OWESOME where we might be surrounded by critics like Tebow has been but nothing can deter us from being OWESOME!
OWESOME where you can become more than you think you can simply because that is who you already *are* in Christ!
OWESOME where you can excel in life simply because you are loved by God!
OWESOME where no one can rob you of this love anymore!
OWESOME where even the antichrist can be transformed to be OWESOME!
OWESOME where we are no longer saying "F*** my life" but we can't help but sing and shout, "I love my life!"
OWESOME where we are loved right where we are!
OWESOME where you can be your true self, who God made you to be!
OWESOME where you can be your true self – your gay self, your colorful self, your broken self, your messed-up self, your woman self, your child self, your seasoned adult self, your transgender self, your political self, your angry self – and the Church, the real Church that I know, will love you for who you are. Every bit of you.

For you are worth it.

GOD.
MADE.
YOU.
TO.

BE.
OWESOME!

1 Corinthians 10:12-13: "You could fall flat on your face as easily as anyone else. Forget about self-confidence; it's useless. Cultivate God-confidence."[35]

When we believe in *this*, we accomplish greater things than we ever thought we could. We witness transformations that bring a smile to our face and our hearts.

We meet people like Carol.

//

Carol is the town crazy. She doesn't shower. She's judgmental. She's pushy. She constantly eats a blended mix of vegetables that looks like baby poop and turns her skin orange. You should stay away from her at all costs.

At least this is what my church members told me when I first came to Reddick.

The first time I met Carol she tried to convince me that I should allow her to have the kids at our church do one of her plays on Easter Sunday. This was Wednesday. Four days before Easter.

When I told her this would be impossible to accomplish, she put her head down and mumbled, *"You don't care about me being a part of your church."*

Did I say this was the first time I met her?

Carol is a church hopper. I knew of at least three churches she had attended besides ours, but there were probably more. She used to be a missionary back in the day but something was definitely a little off with her in her old age. She came to our bible studies sometimes and I couldn't understand what she was saying half the time. Except when she said we needed to convert that Muslim supermarket owner. She was very clear on what she thought about that. There were times, though, when I wasn't sure if she knew what she was saying.

Carol came to our church service once when I was talking about how God made all of us to be OWESOME. I received a phone call from her the next day. Usually she calls me with some advice or to ask if she can have a church directory so she can call and tell everyone "Jesus loves you."

I let her phone call go to voicemail because I just didn't want to hear her ramblings.

Hesitantly, I listened to her message:

"Pastor Russell, thank you so much for your sermon yesterday. I've had a guilt complex all of my life and it was OWESOME to hear that I'm OWESOME. *No one has ever told me I'm OWESOME before.* Thank you so much. God bless you."

I started to look at Carol differently after that. I was preaching a message that *I* needed to start living more.

To preach a gospel with my *actions* as much as my *words*.

To look at Carol the way God looked at her!

Donald Miller – author of *Blue Like Jazz* – puts it this way:

"I pray that every time I meet someone I see Jesus inside of them."[36]

To see even crazy Carol is God's child, uniquely created to be OWESOME.
To see Carol the way God sees her.
To see Jesus is part of her.
To start practicing what I'm preaching.
To show people they're OWESOME like it's the first time they've seen it in their entire lives.

No longer was I annoyed by Carol's unusual answers at bible study because they were her only way to express her faith. She was doing her best to tap into who God made her to be. Even with the baby poop vegetable mix she eats.

God made a loser like Carol – and like you and me – to be OWESOME.

//

And I still listen to Carol's voicemail from time to time.

Because we need to be continually reminded…

WE.
ARE.
OWESOME.

//

OWESOME (pronounced ow • sum) = the ultimate epitomization of being awesome; the confidence one finds from living an exciting, passionate new life in Jesus Christ; awareness and/or discovery of the love & grace of God in everyday life; living to humbly love & serve all people; ex. *"God made you to be OWESOME!", "That mission trip was OWESOME!"*

Chapter 5:
Reading Day

Dream of this
By Marianne Williamson

Our deepest fear is not that we are inadequate.
Our deepest fear is that we are powerful beyond measure.
It is our Light, not our darkness that most frightens us.

We ask ourselves – Who am I to be brilliant, gorgeous, talented,
fabulous?

Actually, who are we not to be?

You are a child of God. Your playing small does not serve the world.
There is nothing enlightened about shrinking so that other people do not
feel insecure around you. We were born to manifest the Glory of God that
is within us. It is not just in some of us, it is in everyone.

And as we let our light shine, we unconsciously give other people
permission to do the same. As we are liberated from our own fears, our
presence automatically liberates others.[37]

//

Reddick Elementary School invited me to Reading Day. This is a day when high school students and adults from different professions come together to read to elementary school students in hopes of encouraging kids to read more. It's a day to share the importance of reading.

They grouped together adults with the high school students to read to each classroom. I was put in a classroom with two high school football players.

The second we entered the classroom I heard screaming:

"*O. My. God!* Look who it is class! Oh, let me get my phone! I have to get your picture to send it to Janice!"

That's right. I'm some kind of famous. She must have heard my preaching.

I looked to my left.

"Oh….. She's excited about the football players."

The teacher was so hysterical about these football players from the high school you would have thought it was Jay-Z and Beyonce.

Reddick groups together with the other small towns around it for one community high school, North Marion High. And on Friday nights in the fall, the entire town turns out to watch the high school football team. Reddick residents live and breathe North Marion football on Fridays and Gator Football on Saturdays.

I pretty much could have walked out of the classroom at that moment and no one would have noticed. The students were all salivating at the direction of their teacher.

"Students, I had these boys in my class when they were your age. Now they are big stars playing for the football team. Tell me, boys, what grades do you need to get to play football?"

"C's ma'am. We need to just have passing grades."

"See, boys and girls! You just need to get C's to play football!"

What did she just say?!

I'm sure you couldn't hide the look of disbelief on my face at that moment. Luckily, no one noticed I was in the room, so it didn't matter.

The high school stars and I each read a book to the students. Then, the teacher stepped out for a minute to brag to the other teachers who was in her classroom.

This was my moment.

"Students, who here is in choir? Who here is in band? Who is in dance? Who here loves math and science? Today is about reading and reading is knowledge. Not everyone here will play football but there are countless other ways you can learn and grow and find your own talents to be someone incredible. So, keep learning and reading. You might even be president someday."

The teacher returned, and we left the room. I shook the hands of the celebrities and promised to never wash my hands ever again. I shall treasure their sweat on my fingers forever. (Eye Roll.)

As I fumbled my way to my car, I was still in disbelief. I was fuming.

C's. C's. C's! So you can pass! To play football"

"Maybe one or two kids in that classroom will play football in high school," I said to myself, "Shouldn't we be teaching them to aspire to be someone greater?! To focus on arts and sciences! I don't know… to *read more* since it's *READING DAY!"*

What happens in our head to tell us we can't aspire to be who we are truly meant to be?

Our context? Where we grew up? Our parents? Our teachers? Discouragement from someone we respect? Failure to achieve our dreams?

When did we stop shooting for the moon and settle for C's? *Or maybe we were never told we could get all A's?*

"Our deepest fear is not that we are inadequate.
Our deepest fear is that we are powerful beyond measure."[37]

We are so much more than C's.

//

While I was trying to process what had happened to me when I left ministry, my wife talked me into seeing a counselor.

I had a mental breakdown one night and I realized I would not be able to get over this without talking to someone. I needed to hear a different perspective and reclaim who I am.

I told the counselor about growing up experiencing the love of God, then dealing with The Bitch, my time in Reddick, enjoying being a pastor, and returning to Texas only to have my calling stripped away from me. After she heard everything in full detail, she asked me:

"Russell, who failed you?"

"The church leaders failed me."

"Yes! You need to remember that! They failed you. *You're not the failure.*"

My friends and family members had been saying the same thing to me for the past three years, but something about having a complete stranger saying that to me made it click.

Thoughts about what had happened to me had been keeping me up all night, then I would crash and not want to do anything. Even though I knew it would be insane to continue on the same path with the United Methodist Church, it still hurt.

I would have some people tell me, "You just need to get over it."

"F*** you!" is what I thought in my head.

When something so big in our lives – that brings us such joy and purpose – is stripped away, we can't help but feel hurt. Or think about what we could have done. Or think about what might have been.

Then my counselor told me to write down all the negative things I say or think about myself in the next week.

That next week I listed off my thoughts or things I said out loud:
- I imagined telling The Bitch off for destroying my career.
- I imagined telling off the cabinet of church leaders for allowing her to destroy my career.
- "I suck as a person" (for sleeping too much and feeling ashamed because I had no motivation).
- Multiple friends were sharing their accomplishments with the ordination process on social media. This really upset me because I realized this was something I would never accomplish myself.
- I kept remembering something an old mentor used to say, "Don't do anything to stand out or raise questions." I was rebelling against the ordination process when he said that. It was partly because I was upset with how The Bitch treated me and how the church leaders slapped my hand and promoted her. I couldn't trust the ordination process anymore because no one stood up for me then and no one was standing up for me now. I refused to fit into a mold of "not asking questions and "not standing out" to respect authority when "authority" bullied me and wouldn't listen.
- I have guilt for not working and not providing for my family.
- I feel like I'm letting my parents and in-law's down.
- I feel like I'm letting down all the churches I've served.
- I feel like I'm letting down all the children who look up to me.
- I feel shame for not making a difference in this world.
- I feel useless.
- I used to think I could do something special but now I am not so sure.
- I feel hurt because my own convictions hurt my career.
- I refused to give up my integrity to fit a certain mold in the church and this got me in trouble.

- I feel like I'm losing hope in people, in general.
- I feel invisible.
- Nobody cares about what I have to say anymore.

After I shared each of these negative thoughts with my counselor, she said:

"So…how do you feel now?"

"Better."

"Why?"

"After writing these down and hearing them out loud, I realized there is another perspective to each of them. There is a perspective I used to believe in and hear about myself, but I've blocked that out. For three years, I've only been able to hear these negative thoughts."

"Now you know what these thoughts are. When you say them again, you can recognize these triggers and tell yourself a different story. Remind yourself there is another perspective."

My counselor then shared a personal story about feeling overweight. She said her friends would make snide comments and she had two options: let those feelings linger or she could make the next step to do something about it. She could go to the gym and work out and eat healthier to make herself feel better, or she could become bitter and not talk to her friends anymore.

My response was, *"OR…you could decide that your friends don't get to decide what type of body weight you should be and decide to be happy with who you are."*

Maybe my counselor was trying to tell me to take the next step to get better or maybe she used some trickery to get me to say what I said.

Maybe she was reminding me to be happy with who I am already. (Maybe both!)

It's not always about taking the next step. But it's definitely not about remaining bitter.

Often, we're already Superman or Superwoman. We're already making so many steps we've surpassed our "step goal" for the day. Our feet hurt because we've been trying to impress everybody and be the best "me" we can be.

Maybe the next step is not doing more. Maybe it's stopping to see we're already superheroes. Maybe the next step is being content with who we are. Believing in ourselves. Being confident in who God made us to be. Being OWESOME. Looking around us and realizing we already have that life we've been looking for. *That maybe you've had superpowers all along.*

True joy is never keeping up with the Joneses or living to make everyone else happy. True joy is being content with who God made you to be.

What our lives look like right now is more than enough to be thankful for.

The laundry might not be done, the house is a disaster, the kids aren't perfect angels, the work is never done, there's always more to do.

But who we are now is more than enough.

You. Are. Enough.

If you are a person of color and you've been told you can't be something because of your skin color, let your color shine. Show the world who you are and what you can do. Don't allow the world to be color blind. Your color is beautiful, and you should be empowered because of who you ARE.

If you are a woman and you've been told you can't be CEO, let your womanhood shine. Show the world who you are and what you can do. Your gender means something powerful and don't let anyone stand in the way of who you ARE.

If you are gay and you've been condemned by your family or church because of who you are, let your rainbow shine. Show the world who you are and what you can do. Your gayness used to mean "happy." Show the bigots you are worth it, and you are a vital part of society. You are not going anywhere! Show the world who you ARE.

If you don't fit into the box the world has laid out for you, break out! Show the world how you live outside the box. You don't fit a certain mold. You define you. You decide what you can do.

Don't let anyone tell you any different.

My friend, Aaron, was told by his guidance counselor in high school he could never graduate from college because he is dyslexic and has A.D.D.

When he graduated from college with a bachelor's degree and two minors, I told him he should smack that diploma on his guidance counselor's desk and say, *"How do you like dem apples?"*

Aaron first believed in himself. He loved and accepted himself, in spite of what his guidance counselor said. And he also took the next step to better himself. He did both.

Today – and every day – find joy in being yourself. Believe you are more than C's.

You are enough. You are more than enough.

//

This, is why representation matters today.

That little boy watching that ISIS propaganda video needs a different song blasting from his stereo.
One that says he can be more than a bearer of terror.
He can be a leader, a caregiver, a superhero,
Where his delusions of grandeur can be a little bit nearer to reality when he looks in the mirror.

Or that gay girl with the nose ring,

Is more than what the news sings.
She's not detestable or molestable,
Or belligerent for protesting a life where she's no longer under the wing of bullying.
There's a new story to tell where she's a leader, a caregiver, a superhero representing to girls around the world that their delusions of grandeur can be a little bit nearer to reality when they look in the mirror.

Don't like that black boy wearing his pants low like a gangster?
Then show him a story where he's typecast as a doctor, a lawyer, a banker.
Where people of color aren't in chains,
Either by slavery, by prison, or low-income pains,
But show them a new story where they can be leaders, caregivers, a superhero representing to people of color all around the world that their delusions of grandeur can be a little bit nearer to reality when they look in the mirror.

You want a world without terror or gangsters?

Then teach them they can be someone different.

We can have women presidents and men dancers and black scientists and gay preachers and brown heroes. Their color, gender, sexuality, or class doesn't define who they can be or can't be.

That being different doesn't make them detestable.
But being different makes a *difference*.

That who they represent is someone that matters.
Someone who is more than C's.
Someone who is no longer invisible.

But stands out in the crowd for all to pay attention to how they are changing the world.
That makes people ask questions because they've never known living this way is possible.
And they never stop asking questions themselves because they know…

They are telling a story no one has told before.

A story they never knew they could tell.

That's why representation matters.

That's why we need teachers to teach children to shoot for the moon.
That's why we need preachers to preach that we are conquerors from
otherwise certain doom.
That's why we need parents to raise their children with love and grace,
so they don't become goons.

Dream of *This*.

//

God made you to be who you already are.

"I can't tell you how much I long for you to enter this wide-open,
spacious life. We didn't fence you in. The smallness you feel comes from
within you. Your lives aren't small, but you're living them in a small
way. I'm speaking as plainly as I can and with great affection. Open up
your lives. Live openly and expansively!" – 2 Corinthians 6:11-13[38]

You are a child of God. *So let your light shine.*

Lose that old life, that old way of thinking about yourself. *And find who*
you truly are.

Love yourself the way God loves you. *Unconditionally.*

Believe you are OWESOME. *Open up your lives.*

See yourself the way God sees you. *For you are wonderfully made.*

I'll see you next Reading Day.

Chapter 6:
The Affirmessy Process

In September 2011, my mother flew in from Texas to visit me and Shannon while we lived in Florida. My Aunt Lettie, my mom's oldest sister, lives in the St. Petersburg area and we went to see her to celebrate her 70th birthday.

All of her children, grandchildren, and great-grandchildren were at her house, as well as my cousin from Washington who surprised all of us for a visit. We had about 20 people crammed into this small, little kitchen enjoying good food and fellowship – just as it happens when most families get together. We were all laughing and sharing stories with each other and making plenty of noise for such a small area.

My uncle was outside. He had nursed this baby squirrel back to health after it had fallen out of a tree. He decided – for reasons that can never be explained – to bring his pet squirrel into this small, little kitchen where 20 people were gathered.

My uncle casually entered with the tiny squirrel on his shoulder to share his accomplishment.

Your ears would start ringing if you heard the screams and squealing.

This made the squirrel freak out. The squirrel jumped up on the ceiling trying to escape the chaos.

The squirrel lost its grip on the ceiling tile and fell on my cousin, John. John is probably the most laid back person you could meet in your life so he just casually brushes the squirrel off his shoulder. So the squirrel returns to the ceiling while everyone else continues to scream.

My cousin, Debbie, was in the process of cutting the birthday cake with the largest kitchen knife known to man. The squirrel again loses its grip on the ceiling and falls on top of my aunt's 70th birthday cake. Debbie starts swinging the knife around like a serial killer to protect herself from the mangy rodent when the squirrel returns to my uncle's shoulders.

"Shut up! Shut up everyone," my uncle insists, "You all are scaring the *squirrel!*"

//

One year in Reddick the church's pianist, Marty, and I attended a Community Maundy Thursday service. I absolutely adore Maundy Thursday because it is the day that happens a few days before Easter where we remember the first communion (also known as The Last Supper).

Even though Jesus is about to betrayed by one of his best friends, Judas, he spends this last evening with his friends washing their feet. He is the definition of being a true master and teacher showing his followers what it looks like to be a leader.

Then he shares a meal with his friends. He knows this will be his last meal with his disciples.

He tells them the bread they are eating is his body. Today we know this represents Jesus giving up his body on the cross, which he will soon do. It represents the nourishment and fulfillment we receive from a life with Christ.

It's more than bread.

When my friend, Sarah, would give the bread to children for communion she would say, *"This means Jesus loves you."*

Like the disciples during their last meal, children like us often don't understand what all this means. Sometimes we just need to hear "This means Jesus loves you."

Then Jesus gave them a cup of wine and said "This is my blood poured out for you and for many for the forgiveness of sins."

It's more than wine.

We're messed up. It doesn't take much to know we stink. We've fallen short of who we are called to be. We've believed the wrong story about ourselves and sought after the wrong things to find fulfillment in our lives.

Just like Judas, who is about to betray Jesus…
And Peter, who will deny he's Jesus' follower when Jesus is on the way to the cross…
And Thomas, who doubts Jesus is real after Jesus is resurrected…
We've also betrayed, denied, and doubted Jesus is the real deal.

But Jesus knows everything about us. He knows we're messed up. And he still washes our feet and gives up his body and blood for us.

He still meets us in this mess.

He still offers the bread and wine. He still gives up his body and blood. He offers this Holy Communion that represents his relationship with us. This bread and juice are an outward symbol of an inward grace which heals us, liberates us, transforms us, molds us, guides us, nourishes us, fulfills us, loves us, unites us, and affirms us in this mess we've made.[39]

As Marty and I attend this community Maundy Thursday service, it's not exactly the holy moment reminding us of this relationship that I was hoping to experience.

We were looking around thinking, *"Is this really what God had in mind?"*

Marty and I were trying not to make eye contact because we just wanted to laugh at the predicament we found ourselves in.

It was obvious our piano player for the service had never heard of these songs before. Like ever. I'm talking about "The Old Rugged Cross" and "When I Survey the Wondrous Cross" and traditional Lent songs. One of the other pastors and I were forced to lead the congregation in singing. He addressed the congregation: "You know if the two of us are leading the singing something is wrong."

I mean, this church had as much rhythm as Steve Martin in *The Jerk*[40]

Marty and I drove together to the service and when we returned to her car afterwards, we both breathed out a sigh of relief. We paused in silence to fully take in what we had just experienced.

Then in unison we both cried out: *"What. Was. That?!"*

"Look," I sputtered out, "When Jesus was preparing to die, was he thinking 2000 years later we would honor and remember him by…*whatever the hell that was?!"*

Marty, as she continued both laughing and shaking her head, said, "No one is ever going to believe us when we tell them just how miserable this service was! That was the most miserable service I have been to in my life, Russell!"

"I know how the book of Lamentations was written now. It was written after they were all lamenting about suffering from sitting in *that* worship service! My goodness!"

Marty asked, "Ok, Pastor Russell, there has to be some sort of lesson here that we are supposed to learn. What is it?"

I replied, "When planning a worship service, *don't do it like that.* Ever."

"EVER!"

Marty and I laughed all the way back to our church.

//

Squirrels and miserable worship. We have to laugh at the mess we've made.

It's funny to think we ever desired perfection. We expect a life with God to be glamorous. A life with God will take away all our pain and make our children angels and our families perfect. We will be showered with money and all our prayers will be answered. And certainly our worship will represent this holy, magnificent experience every time.

But a life with God instead puts us in the middle of a muddy, disgusting pit. We're sitting with other disgusting people who we would never have sat with before. And our lives are nowhere near perfect. Our lives are still a mess.

Our worship is still miserable. Like Jesus, our friends are about to betray us and we'll be sent to suffering on the cross. Like my family, our celebration is about to be interrupted by a rodent and the birthday cake will be ruined.

And it's a moment we will never forget.

It's a moment when we are brought together as a family. To laugh at our imperfections. To smile at our silliness. To find something holy amongst something so miserable.

A beautiful mess.

//

Our choir director just threatened to leave the church. Our chair of trustees reminded me we need to follow church polity and tradition of the church or we're going to hell in a handbasket. Tensions are rising because our new, passionate young leaders asked to do something different and the long-time leaders are not having it.

"This is the way we've always done it."

The young leaders' passion is quickly diminishing. They are about ready to give up if this is what church leadership looks like.

I'm sure every church leader has been here.

Those dreaded church board meetings where everyone is at each other's throats. Things get heated and the church is seemingly beyond repair.

As our church in Reddick started to grow, we had a wonderful problem.

The "kids" – the adults under 50 – were becoming leaders in the church. As it is for younger, excited leaders, they were ready to make things happen. To get things done. They were ready to start new ministries for the church at full speed. They were ready to do all the work until the work was complete. And to get started *today*.

As they presented their intentions to our seasoned leaders, the experienced ones were like "hold the motors, kids." *This* is the process we take to make things happen. One has to do this and this and this and this. You have to get all ministries approved by us first. *"This is the way we've always done it."* This is our tradition. And you're not going to change things now.

Toes felt stepped on from all sides. Excitement was deflated. Feelings were hurt. And something had to be done before things got worse.

//

One of the greatest mentors I ever had was the late Dr. Ken Diehm, who died unexpectedly of leukemia in 2011. In a world full of boring, white pastors, Ken was the exception. He had a way of engaging people I had never seen before. He had a way of expressing this peaceful aura and calmly pulling us into his stories.

And he laughed so much. I'll never forget his laugh.

If he was talking to you, you were the only person in the room. He gave you such respect and because of that he earned the respect of everyone.

Ken would talk to me about having a "blended" worship service. In a church that had been battling how to keep the old, traditional values that makes church a church and learning how to adapt to a younger generation who seeks something new and fresh and creative for today, Ken created the best of both worlds.

He would not forget the older generation and their values. He would welcome aspects of traditional worship to remind us where we came from. And how these old, old stories were still important for us today.

And he would think of new, creative ways to engage an over-stimulated group of young adults. He used projectors to engage the congregation in his teachings. He welcomed new songs, but sometimes they were old, traditional songs the seasoned members would remember which were expressed in new, fresh ways.

This blended worship service honored every generation. It was worship for everyone. *And it worked.*

Every year he did his infamous Super Bowl commercial sermon. Everyone looked forward to it every year. He would analyze the most popular Super Bowl commercials and explain how the underlying message behind each of them taught us a lesson (or how the bible shows us a different perspective than what we saw on television). His sermons and his worship were so creative and vibrant.

He was creating something new for today that was a joy to watch and be a part of.

//

As I thought about all of my church leaders, I realized they simply didn't understand one another. I called them back for a special board meeting a week later to try and repair our broken, deflated leadership.

We talked about bridging the generational gap. We discussed our differences in leadership styles.

We talked about respecting the old doctrine and traditions of the church. The seasoned leaders had value in how they have been here before. They had the experience of running the church, allowing them to be mentors to our younger leaders and help them understand the process of making things happen properly for the church.

And we talked about encouraging the passionate, new excitement of our younger leaders. The younger leaders had the energy and strength to make things happen where our seasoned leaders just didn't have the bodies to do the work as well anymore. The seasoned leaders could take a break from the work load while mentoring the young leaders on how to accomplish the church work correctly.

Yes, we will see some changes happening to our old church but that is how we know our church is alive! We're adapting to a newer generation while not forgetting our older, wiser generation!

Once we had this discussion to understand our differences, my God! This leadership working together was a beautiful thing to watch.

We affirmed the mess we were in. And instead of shying away from it, we met each other in our mess and created something blended and beautiful.

Occasionally I would walk in the sanctuary during the week and find two generations of leaders working together to complete a task and it made my heart happy. This is what Jesus wanted from communion, from that last meal with his followers. To bring completely different, equally messed-up people together to work together as a church, as family. To be the body of Christ.

Like my mentor before me, we created something new for today that was such a joy to be a part of.

//

The Affirmessy Process – The thought that life is a journey – or process – which affirms the multiple realities of all people and allows for messy conversations, messy theology, messy questions, and messy understanding. The journey in this *affirmessy process* is not about having all the answers, but rather the "answer" is enjoying/allowing/affirming each other's asking of the messy – sometimes unsolvable – questions.

//

One of my professors in seminary encouraged us to come up with a new word. This was my word: *affirmessy*.

It was birthed out of the time I was working with The Bitch. Believing something meaningful could happen out of this messy, disgusting, confusing time was hard to keep ahold of.

I almost left the ministry because I didn't understand why I was being scolded for standing up to a bully.

At the Walk to Emmaus, a spiritual retreat that reminds us of God's infinite love, I remembered who I am called to be. At the end of the retreat, you share what you learned during that time. I shared my story of how I was reminded of who I am in God in Jesus in the Holy Spirit and how I needed to stop listening to all the wrong voices.

Another pastor in the room whom I had never met walked up to me afterwards, introduced herself, and said:

"You don't know me but I worked for (The Bitch) before too. I want you to know that everything she says has everything to do with her and it has nothing to do with you."

The Bitch had told my wife about the "horrors" of being a pastor, and how it takes such a commitment to go where the church leads that she will divorce her husband if he doesn't stay committed to her call as a pastor.

This caused great concern for my wife because she was very committed to her career, as well.

I told Shannon, "I don't care what she said! Just because I am in ministry doesn't mean my career trumps yours. Whenever an opportunity arises for either one of us, we will discuss it as a couple. I work for God, you come second, and the church comes third."

So when Shannon had an opportunity to move to Florida for her career we did.

Through that mess of working with The Bitch, it eventually led me to move to Florida to have the time of my life as the pastor of Reddick United Methodist Church. And to show my wife that our love always comes first. That mess led me to something so magical it changed my life for the better forever.

The affirmessy process is seeing a different perspective beyond our miserable lives and messy situations.

I've seen the affirmessy process when divorced persons set aside their differences to work together for the love of their children.

I've seen this when Christians set aside their convictions to love someone wholly and completely even when they don't agree with their lifestyle.

I've seen this when people choose to forgive someone who has wronged them, to actively show grace to someone who does not deserve it.

I've seen this when political activists set aside their Republican or Democrat views to work together for a community in need.

I've seen this when leaders of different backgrounds, personalities, and styles work together for the good of everyone.

I've seen this when leaders have stopped what they are doing to treat someone like he/she is the only person in the room.

When we truly listen to someone else's messed up story, we can't help but learn something ourselves.

Sometimes it's just better to listen because we always have room to grow.

There's always a need to keep adapting on this journey we call life.

There's always a bigger picture than the messy situation right in front of us.

//

The affirmessy process is loving people right where they are.

We all have friends who have betrayed us. We have annoying uncles interrupting family gatherings with their pet squirrels. We have leaders and co-workers we don't understand. We have churches who have no rhythm or talent whatsoever. We have churches who are not doing what they are supposed to.

We have friends like Carol who eat baby poop vegetable mix who are still a part of our messed up family.

But everyone needs to know they're OWESOME. Everyone needs a hand to hold. A chair to sit in. And someone to sit with.

Sometimes it's better to sit and listen to those we disagree with. To set aside our differences and enjoy each other's presence in this mess.

Sometimes it's simply better to be *loving* than to be *right*.

Jesus lived this better than anyone. Instead of condemning us for our broken, messed-up lives, he sat with us in our mess. He ate with the outcasts and tax collectors and prostitutes. He held the hands of the sick and dangerous. He welcomed the thief and sinner into His kingdom.

As the band Relient K once put it in their song, "Failure to Excommunicate":

"He loved the ones the world just loves to hate."[41]

Jesus transformed his miserable last supper into something beautiful when he died on the cross and was resurrected three days later.

He transformed our mess. He loved us in it. He loves us even when the world hates us. He made something perfect out of our imperfections. And he continues to make something beautiful out of all of us.

It's perfect…even when it's not.

He took our miserable, confusing, laughable, sometimes disgusting, messed-up worship. And said, *"This is good."*

This is holy.
This is sacred.

This. This moment has been set apart as something meaningful.

We have been affirmed in our mess. That's *affirmessy*.

Chapter 7:
The Mutant Problem[42]

When I was in college at Texas Wesleyan University, I was one of two guys in the Theatre Department who was known for being a Christian.

One day an older gentleman stood in between the Theatre building and the Art building screaming at the top of his lungs.

"All theatre majors are going to hell! All art majors are going to hell! If you are a theatre major, you are gay and you are going to hell!"

He was a mighty pleasant individual. The art majors had a joyous time dressing up like dogs and giving this guy a hard time. Some people – like myself – tried to talk some sense into this guy but he was convinced we were all going to hell.

I was a young youth minister and I didn't like this guy representing God so I went upstairs to the computer lab and pulled up a story I knew that talked about God's forgiveness.

When I returned to the crazy evangelist, I encouraged the crowd gathered around him to come over to me to "hear the real truth." I read aloud the story I found, then told them about God's forgiveness and love and grace.

"This is the *real* message! God loves you where you are! Don't believe this junk this guy is trying to say to you!"

The man was yelling louder as I was talking, which only caused me to talk louder. As I was closing up my message, he sang "Amazing Grace" then returned to his car and left.

The crowd dispersed. My buddy, Jesse, ran into the theatre building screaming at the top of his lungs:

"Guess what everybody?! Russell got rid of the fake religion guy! *Russell got rid of the fake religion guy!*"

//

A fellow member in Theatre asked me, as God's representative, what God thought about him being gay.

I responded, "God loves you."

He said, "Ok. But what does God think about me being gay?"

I repeated myself, "God loves you more than anyone."

He said, "Yes, but what does God think about me being gay?"

Our conversation continued like a broken record for a few more minutes until he gave up because I wasn't giving him the answer he was looking for.

I wanted him to know that God loves him. But he wanted to know that God *accepted* him.

For my friend, loving someone but not accepting someone's lifestyle was just as bad as not loving them. Being gay is his identity, and not to accept his identity, is to reject him altogether.

The phrase "loving the sinner, but hating the sin" was just a cop-out not to accept him for who he is.

For my friend – and for gay people like him – if being gay is a sin then that means who they are is, in itself, a sin, and they don't want to be in relationship with a *God* or a *church* that thinks their very identity is a sin.

We might as well be telling them they are going to hell on the street corner.

//

The comic book superhero group called the X-men is a group of mutants who are outcasts by society because they are "different." They each have superpowers because of a genetic mutation, but the humans don't consider this mutation to be a gift or a superpower. It is more of a threat and a curse.

In the beginning of the first *X-men*[43] movie, we see the United States government trying to decide what to do with "The Mutant Problem." They are looking for a cure to the mutations. It's as if humans are the norm and mutants are a problem to be eliminated. Any reasonable person would call this genocide.

One senator wants the government to find every mutant and decide whether they should be given a license to live or not since some of them are definitely a danger to society.

Jean Grey, who is secretly a mutant herself, responds: "We give people a license to drive a car. We don't give people a license to *live*."

But we have seen this time and time again in the real world.

The Nazis sought to eliminate the Jews for not being the chosen people of society.
The Ku Klux Klan wanted to eliminate black people for not being the chosen race.
Americans put all Japanese people in camps to protect America from a Japanese threat.
There are "Christian" camps to "pray away the gay" in young persons' lives.
Donald Trump has recently put a ban on transgender persons in the military.

There is even Westboro Baptist Church in Topeka, Kansas, whose members protest at military funerals because they claim that soldiers are dying because America has become more tolerant of gay people and God is mad at us. Thus, soldiers are dying because America loves gay people and God hates that. Excellent logic, don't you think?

To us, many of these groups seem crazy and unreasonable, but I am positive that every, single one of us deals with our own stereotypes and prejudices and discrimination.

An older family friend once tried to convince me that I should hate black people because he was once in Africa and he witnessed these "savages" murder people in cold blood. He said, "You just don't understand. All black people are ruthless killers just like this. And none of them can be trusted."

On the flip side, when I was a youth minister I was having a discussion about race with the students. One particular student – a freshman in high school – said, "A stereotype is thinking that one person or a group of people of a certain race, sexuality, etc. is one way so every person of that race, sexuality, etc. is the same way."

This freshman in high school gets it. This boy grew up to become the student body president at the University of Oklahoma (and may become president of the United States of America one day).

//

In the 2nd *X-men* movie, *X2: X-men United*[44], there is an insane military colonel named William Stryker who is trying to eliminate this mutant problem. He wants to wipe out every, single one of them. In the movie, he is a military colonel. But do you know what he is in the comic books? A Christian minister.

Does this say something about how the outside world views Christians? Are we seen as uninformed, unreasonable people ready to make stereotypical, snap judgments against an entire group of people?

According to the book *UnChristian*[45], by David Kinnaman and Gabe Lyons, yes we are.

UnChristian presents research by the Barna Group, which examined why young people are leaving the church.

The top 3 perceptions that these young persons had of Christians were:
(1) Judgmental
(2) Hypocritical, and…
(3) Antihomosexual

I know this is true because I've watched many church members post their prejudices on social media today.

One friend, Andrew[46], and I were discussing the disgusting cow dung that has been flung all over social media.

"How can they talk this way? Is it just because it's behind a keyboard in their room at their house that they are expressing how they really feel?"

"But is it how they *really* feel? I *know* these people," Andrew replied, "If the people they are condemning were on their doorsteps asking for a warm meal and a place to stay, they would love them. They would welcome them into their home as their honored guest. But then I look at what they are say on social media thinking, *'Who are you?!'* Who they are on social media is not the loving Christian person I know them to be."

Is social media showing who we truly are? Or is our true self the person who greets anyone and everyone with a smile, seeking to love people where they are?

I mean, the church is supposed to be this place for the outcasts but instead it's become a place for a bunch of entitled pricks who hold their noses up at anyone who tries to ask them to change into something different. The world is mutating but the church is calling this a problem and condemning the culture around them.

I've heard it said that maybe God places different people here on this earth to see how we treat them.

If that's true, we have failed God's test.

//

The LGBT community is better at loving the outcasts than the Church! Churches can criticize the gay community all day but the gay community is loving students who have considered suicide when the church is often the cause of it! The gay community is welcoming the broken while the church is condemning them. The gay community is creating a new message of love today while churches are fading into to the background like a crazy, judgmental uncle.

Anne Lamott says, "You can safely assume you've created God in your own image when it turns out that God hates all the same people you do."[47]

In other words, God's love goes beyond the people you might love and accept. Your enemies are not God's enemies. Your prejudices are not God's prejudices. Your perspective is not God's perspective.

If you think you have God and the bible all figured out, then God is certainly made in your own image.

If you meet a pastor who has all the answers, run! God is God and we are not. There are just some questions where we don't have the answer. And that is ok. It is better to ask the questions and walk with people on their journey than condemn them because we think we know all there is to know about *their* lives.

We're not the judge. We're the sheep called to follow the shepherd. We're called to care for our flock and *love* those around us.[48]

//

We should realize that when Jesus came to the earth, he tried to set the tone for how we should treat people. Jesus accepted the people everyone else rejected. And he accepted them without condition.

Jesus became a scapegoat for some of the religious leaders who wanted to persecute him for being different. Jesus did things that no one had seen before and some people saw him as a threat. You could say Jesus was seen as a mutant.

A group of people decided to crucify Jesus to make an example out of him. But this crucifixion only exposed the evil prejudices that some people had and the unwarranted power that the wrong people had.

Stan Lee, the creator of the Marvel Superheroes said in 1968:

"Let's lay it right on the line. Bigotry and racism are among the deadliest social ills plaguing the world today. But, unlike a team of costumed supervillains, they can't be halted with a punch in the snoot, or a zap from a ray gun. The only way to destroy them is to expose them – to reveal them for the insidious evils they really are."[49]

Jesus should have been the scapegoat to remove any other person or group from becoming scapegoats in the future. But we're still persecuting minorities and others who are a little different today.

If we don't want Christians to be seen as judgmental, anti-homosexual, and hypocritical, maybe it's time we show something different than these prejudices. Maybe it's time we stand with these outcasts. Maybe it's time we become an advocate for them.

We're not being persecuted as Christians with any comparison to that of people of color or homosexuals. No one questions your humanity or condemns you to hell for your lifestyle. No one starts a movement for "Christian lives matter" because you haven't had to talk to your children about how they need to keep their mouth shut around people of power so they come home alive.

Your faith doesn't hate you simply for who you are.

Your faith serves a man named Jesus who exposed the injustices of this world so all people could know they are children of God.

//

A friend of mine – who I respect as one of the most profound, passionate, loving, all-around best Christians I know – has natural, bright red hair.

When we were in high school, he hung out with who most people would call "punks." But this group of people – although they dressed different than the norm – were some of the nicest people I knew. My friend had a mohawk that he spiked up for school, but on Sunday he always left it flat for church.

One Sunday, though, we were up all night for prom and he had his bright, red mohawk spiked up for church.

And he just so happened to be giving a testimony in front of everyone at church that Sunday.

The pastor received numerous complaints about this punk kid speaking in front of the church with a Mohawk. The pastor defended this student, thankfully, but it is one of those moments that make you say, "*Really?!*"

These church members were more concerned about this punk kid's Mohawk than the fact that he was sharing his faith in front of hundreds of people! This punk kid was up all night for prom, and he was not just *in* church, but was *speaking* to the entire church about his *faith*! *And we have a problem with his Mohawk?! Really?!*

//

Since the *UnChristian* book came out revealing the perceptions that young people have of the church, there has been a movement to change some of these perceptions. I was once at a meeting for leaders in the church where this was the particular topic. As they started talking about their goals to reach young people, there was an uproar from the young people in the room stating there were no young people seated on their board to reach young people! How would they know how to reach young people without any young people helping them to know how to reach them?!

In an act of spontaneity, one of the speakers had all the young people come up on stage to be recognized. He tried to show all the people there how young people are a presence in our churches. But I think we all know that bringing a group on stage is one thing, and making them a leader or member of a committee is another thing.

If we want to know how to reach gay persons or persons of color or women or young people, then we need to hear the voices of those in the trenches. They need to teach *us* how we can be the Church.

//

I'm seriously unqualified to write about gay persons or persons of color or women. You want to know their stories? Talk to them. Spend time with them. Make them leaders for change.

You want to know what young people think? Talk to them!
You want to know how to remove some of your stereotypes of people of color? Get to know them!
You want to change your prejudice of gay people? Ask them questions about their lives! Learn their stories!

Rev. Sue Haupert-Johnson, a bishop for the United Methodist Church, once said at a clergy meeting, "*It's hard to have prejudices when you're in relationship.*"

I know my perspective of gay persons has changed because I have become friends with many of them. One of my seminary professors, Dr. Stephen Sprinkle, is gay and he encouraged me and supported me when I needed it the most. I will always support gay persons in church leadership because of him. I will defend gay rights and accept gay persons and welcome them into our church and love and accept them for who they are because they are my friends.

I know some people still don't believe in women pastors. But for me, some of the greatest pastoral influences I had as a kid and a teenager were women pastors. I wouldn't be the same if it weren't for the great, Godly women pastors that helped shape my spiritual journey.

Some of you have had bad experiences with a particular pastor, but please don't think that because you may not have liked one pastor of a certain gender or race (or being a pastor in general) that all pastors are that way.

The X-men had many X-women like Jean Grey, Rogue, Storm, and Kitty Pride, who were seen as equal to their male counterparts.

The Gospel of Luke shows how Jesus included and respected women with the disciples. As the Gospels show, if it weren't for the women weeping at the tomb, we would not have even known about the resurrection. Some people – jokingly or not – try to blame women for original sin because of the apple in the Garden of Eden, but if it were not for women we would not know of Jesus' resurrection and how our sin has been erased by the power of the resurrection![50]

//

Instead of holding negative perceptions of a person or a group of people, we should seek to get to know them. I promise you your prejudices will be removed once you're open to being friends with them and accepting whoever this person is for you.

And the truth is: there will be some people with whom you do not agree with and do not particularly like. There are still villains in this world who create negative perceptions of a group of people who are different from them.

What if I said, "I had bad service from one waiter at one restaurant so I am going to treat every waiter poorly from now on"? You would probably call me a jerk.

If I were to say, "One Christian I met said I was going to hell so all Christians are judgmental," we should all agree that this is an invalid, illogical argument.

Besides, I got rid of the fake religion guy.

I know that many perceptions people have of Christians are not the reality of the loving, accepting people I know or all the churches I have been a part of. None of our churches are perfect, though, and there *are* prejudices in *every* church. But we're all still growing. We're still exposing the truth of the Gospel that Jesus tried to show us over 2000 years ago, and learning how to live like Jesus today.

Pastor and author Lillian Daniels says, "*I am tired of apologizing for a church I am not a part of.*"[51]

Let us strive to show the next gay person or black person or atheist or Muslim or young person we meet that the perceptions they might have of us is not who we actually are.

And let us strive to love and *accept* them just for being a child of God.

Let us appreciate our differences.

In a world that loves stereotypes and prejudices and generalizations, let us be the exception to the rule.

//

I was at Disney World once with Shannon and my sister-in-law and her husband and their kids. We had stopped to take a breath for a moment. I glanced at my phone and saw that it was 2:00 on the dot.

Off to the side where not many people could see, there were a couple of Muslims who had pulled out their prayer blankets and were stopping to pray at the top of the hour like most Muslims do.

I thought, "How cool is that?" What an example of faith and a commitment to prayer they have! I stopped to say a prayer myself as I appreciated their commitment to their faith in the middle of such a place as Disney world.

//

One of the X-men, Nightcrawler, is solid blue all over his body and he was actually a priest at one point in the comic book.

In *X2: X-men United*, he talks about how people used to look at him differently when he was in the circus.

Nightcrawler said:

"You know, outside the circus, most people were afraid of me. But I didn't hate them. I pitied them. Do you know why? Because most

people will never know anything beyond what they see with their own two eyes."[52]

Don't be afraid of the people you don't know. Get to know them. Educate yourself of their differences and learn to appreciate them for who they are. You might find more in common with that person you thought was "so different" than you think.

You might learn that those people you hate in the outside culture actually have a lot to teach us about love. You might learn that their stories are worth telling. You might hear how their friends have been condemned and persecuted for who they are and they need a place to call home. A place that loves them where they are. A place that teaches them they've been created to be OWESOME because no one has told them that before!

You might learn that there is neither Jew nor Gentile, neither slave nor free, neither male and female, neither young or old, neither heterosexual or homosexual, neither white, black, or other people of color, neither American or un-American, neither Christian or unchristian....[53]

For we are all one in Christ Jesus.

//

I have a dream for the church. I dream of gay couples with their children being a part of the everyday life of the church. I dream of lesbian pastors preaching God's word like my friend, Carrie, does. I dream of people proclaiming, "I thank God for making you a lesbian, for standing up for those like you to show them a world where they are loved and accepted for who they are."

I dream of the church standing with the gay students who have contemplated suicide. I have a dream the church will cry with them; not be the reason they are crying. I have a dream that the church will no longer condemn them, but will accept them as children of God and help them tell a different story about themselves.

I dream of a church where gay persons are a part of marriage classes at the church just like everyone else. I see a church where the love of married gay persons is seen just like the love of their heterosexual friends. I see a church that will baptize their kids and help raise them as a church just like any other kids.

I dream of a church where the culture around us is nothing to be feared or condemned, but a city of people to be loved. I see a church that listens to the stories of our culture and realizes they need a new story to tell. I see a church that is a vast, diverse rainbow of colorful people! I see a church where the leaders represent this diversity. I see a place where we can learn something from the voices in the trenches we've never allowed ourselves to listen to before.

I see a church where there is a place for all of our emptiness. There is healing for all of our pain. There is a home for all of our families. There is help for all of our hurt.

There is no cure for the mutant problem.

The mutants are one of us. They're part of our culture and our lives and they're never going away.

And they can be a part of the church.

They can be a part of love's story.

I dream of that day.

Chapter 8:
Bud

If you were to ask me to prove to you that God does *not* exist, I might tell you about how the universe is filled with darkness.

I might tell you about the countless planets and stars that are just out there with no life whatsoever.

I might tell you that Earth is one, little planet amongst this big, big universe and only a small portion of life exists here.

Why would a Creator design this entire universe and only allow life to blossom in one little area?

And not to mention, everything that lives on this small, little planet after a period of time…*dies*!

In the meantime, we suffer. We sometimes create death ourselves sooner than expected by murdering one another. Sometimes these life forces inflict endless amounts of pain on one another. Sometimes we grow to experience a little bit of life and joy… and then it's ripped away from us.

We experience grief over the loss of life that we were able to enjoy for only a brief period of time.

Why?

Why do we have a life this short surrounded by years and years of death and darkness?

//

When I was about to move back to Texas from Florida, I went on a house hunting trip. One thing I was not looking forward to experiencing again was the traffic.

Every, single highway is under construction and the traffic is *unbelievable*!

As I was driving up Gainesville road from my home to get to Reddick – driving by the horse farms and the beautiful, peaceful landscaping – I began to feel resentment.

Why do I have to go back to that traffic? Why did I only get to drive by these horse farms for a few years? Why am I going back to that construction and mess?

Then, I realized something. I had stopped enjoying the time I have left driving by these horse farms.

Instead of the peace and serenity I usually feel driving by these horse farms, I only complained about the *"why's"* and the *"why me's."*

Instead of enjoying the moments I had left, I was feeling resentment towards it.

//

If you were to ask me to prove to you that God *exists*, I might tell you again about how the universe is filled with darkness.

I might tell you about the countless planets and stars that are just out there with no life whatsoever.

I might tell you that Earth is one, little planet amongst this big, big universe and only a small portion of life exists here.

Then, I might remind you that in spite of all this darkness, there *is* life here.

Why would a Creator design this entire universe and only allow life to blossom in one little area?

Because life here is important. Life here means something.

Yes, it's true. As Billy Graham says, "One in one person will *die.*"

But because of our Creator, because of our Savior… *life is eternal.*

Because of our Creator, because of our Savior… *we truly live!*

Here. And now.

We *will* suffer. We will experience pain. We will grieve the loss of life. But for a time, we experience *endless amounts of joy*.

We grieve because we love.[54]

Would we rather to have never known of that love we felt with that special person in our lives? Would we rather have never had that special time in our lives? We grieve because we love.

And we should be so thankful for the love and life we had even for that brief moment.

We'll never forget that joy we shared during that brief moment on our journey of life.

Nothing can take away those moments of love we shared together.

God exists because – even for that brief moment on that small, little planet in the vast, incredible universe – there was life, there was light, there was love.

//

The 5 stages of grief are:
  (1) Denial
  (2) Anger
  (3) Bargaining
  (4) Depression
  (5) Acceptance

The 5 stages of grief are pretty well-known. Even if you haven't heard of them before, if you have experienced grief before I think you would agree these emotions are pretty common during our grief.

We all experience denial and shock for a while when we experience bad news. Then, when it finally hits us we become angry. Then we try to bargain with God to change the outcome we've experienced. Then depression kicks in for a while when we think there is no hope.

Then, finally, we're able to accept our life change and we're ready to keep on living.

//

I want to add a sixth stage of grief.

Beyond acceptance.

It might be called that moment *after* grief.

That moment where you decide grief isn't going to affect you anymore.

I'd call it the Inspiration stage or Creativity stage or the "I-got-my-energy-back" stage.

It's that moment where you don't just feel like life moves on – it's not just accepting the new life you have – it's that moment you feel like it's time for you to *create new life*.

The Creativity Stage.

It's not that the other stages of grief ever go away fully. We sometimes never stop grieving the loss of a loved one or a lost relationship or job or an idea or the way things used to be. We sometimes never lose sight of a past memory we wish was still a reality.

But in this sixth stage, we are ready to create a new reality for us and for the people around us.

We're ready to connect to those who might be grieving like us and help them through their grieving process.

//

One of the biggest changes we tackled in Reddick while I was there for a few years was the change in music to reach out to the newer generations in our church.

The biggest critic to this change in music was Bud Cowart.

Bud is an *acquired taste*.

At first, he's bitter. You want to spit that horrible, stubborn taste out.

The worse he tastes; the more he tries to get under your skin. If he sees you're disturbed by him, he gives you hell even more.

Whatever you do, do not show him signs of weakness. Do not let him see that he's getting to you or he will be on you like a spider monkey.

Bud was the most stubborn pain in the ass ever.

The people he loved the most…he drove absolutely insane!

He was the biggest control freak. He always had to have things his way.

And he was not spontaneous. He didn't like anything new. He did not like to be surprised.

If his four daughters forgot to tell him about a lunch or event we were having at church, he wouldn't come. He had to plan ahead for what he was going to do that day or he just wasn't doing it.

He didn't listen to *anything* you said. But he told you *everything* that was on his mind.

He complained about the damn music *Every. Single. Week.*

And he hated to sing! For someone that didn't sing, he sure had an opinion about whatever everyone else sang!

Every Sunday, Bud wouldn't be afraid to tell me, "*Well, I just didn't care for that damn loud music!*"

It came to the point where I started to get really annoyed with Bud complaining about the music every Sunday.

//

But then I talked to a colleague and friend of mine about Bud complaining every Sunday. He explained to me about how every change we experience in our lives results in grief just like if we lost a loved one.

My colleague said to me, "It's probably not just that Bud doesn't like the new music; it's that he's grieving the loss of not hearing the music he likes."

This change resulted in him grieving the loss of the way things used to be.

When my colleague gave me this insight it changed the way I looked at Bud. While I wanted him to accept this new music for the younger generations in our church, I didn't want him to think that what he wanted wasn't still important.

This is so important. While we were reaching out to younger generations, and helping the different generations understand each other, it was also important not to forget our older generation. To still make them feel worth it.

So, I started playing the Statler brothers, his favorite band. I didn't play it because I cared for it but because I cared for Bud. I wanted him to know he still mattered to this church.

After we played the Statler brothers one Sunday, he had the biggest grin after church as he walked up to greet me. He proudly stood there waiting for his turn to talk.

"Bud, are you happy now?!" I said to him before he got his chance to gloat.

"Did you see the way they were tapping their feet to that music?" Bud boasted, *"See, I know what I'm talking about, preacher!"*

//

For those of us that *really* knew Bud, there was a layer deep down. I'm talking like *way* deep down. Underneath his grumpy face and annoying attitude. Beneath his bald head and wrinkly, old skin...

There was a man with the *biggest* heart.

//

But let me back up a little bit. There is a reason Bud is a little crazy. I didn't realize what it was until I visited him at the hospital after he busted open his head and had to get staples.

There is a reason he's crazy that I noticed after I spent a couple hours with him and his daughters.

His girls were trying to convince me to watch this show, *Duck Dynasty*[55]. If you haven't seen *Duck Dynasty*, it's this reality show of a bunch of rednecks who do stupid stuff all the time. They argue with each other. They get mad at each other. They pull pranks on one another... and they're family.

And I'm watching his daughters interact with their dad. They are yelling at him for driving himself to the hospital. They are trying to get this stubborn, old man to quit making jokes and listen to them.

And I don't think I've ever laughed so hard at the hospital.

I told them, "*Forget Duck Dynasty. You all need your own reality show!*"

And I realized Bud has an excuse for being crazy. *His four daughters made him that way*!

I know they'll tell you it's *his* fault. Which is also true. They're *all* to blame.

//

The truth is he loved his daughters and grandchildren with everything he had. They each had his heart, his wit, his stubbornness, his strength, and his humor.

Bud and his late wife, Florence, taught their girls that they had to attend church until they were 18. Unless they were dying, they went to church.

Bud had lunch every Sunday after church with his girls. He mastered the art of listening to them. He would allow them to argue about a subject for a little bit, and then he would say, "*Ok, it's time to turn the page.*"

I looked forward to our fellowship time every Sunday morning at church. As soon as Bud walked through the doors everyone screamed, "*Hey Bud! Hey Bud!*"

He would quietly reply "Hey," as he kept walking to get his morning coffee. He would try to keep that grumpy look on his face, but if you were paying attention, he always had a little bit of a smile to see us.

He would do his best to drive me crazy after that – and anyone else who would allow him to.

Then, Sophie, his granddaughter would walk in. With such great affection for her grandpa, she would always shower him with kisses on his bald head. Bud would say, "*Now quit that!*" And he would do his best to drive his granddaughter crazy like the rest of us.

But then if you were paying attention, he always had the biggest smile for Sophie.

Bud would try to hide it, but he might have had the biggest heart of us all.

//

I told all these stories and more at Bud's funeral.

Once I attended a funeral where the best friend of the deceased person was giving the eulogy. During the entire eulogy, the friend preached at people to "get their lives right." Not once did this friend mention the person who just died.

Your best friend just died and all you can do is preach at people?!

Since the very first funeral service I conducted as pastor, I lived by this philosophy:

I will preach the gospel at a memorial service, but I will preach the gospel by remembering this person's life and how he/she taught us to live better lives.

This was the same philosophy I had for Bud's service. I warned his daughters I wasn't going to shy away from who Bud really was. They said, "*Go for it!*"

Some people said it was the greatest funeral they had ever been to. Greatest funeral? Those two words don't seem to go together. But we laughed and laughed and laughed in memory of Bud.

We remembered him for who he was – all of him. And we thanked God for the time we got to spend with this stubborn, old man.

See beyond this stubborn man was someone who made large, anonymous donations to individuals in need. He would help out families when they needed it the most. His family told me he was quick to lend a helping hand when he was younger. He never hesitated to share the harvest from his farm with his neighbors.

If we had more men like stubborn, old Bud, we might all have enough food to eat.

//

There's a story in the third chapter of the book of Ezra[56] where they are rebuilding a church temple.

As the builders lay the foundation of the new temple, they celebrate with trumpets and cymbals and vestments, singing, praising, and giving thanks to the Lord for "he is good and his steadfast love endures forever."

The scripture says that all the people responded with praise because the foundation of the Lord was laid.

But there were also many priests and Levites and heads of the family, old people who had seen the first temple and its foundations, and they *wept* with a loud voice when they saw the new temple.

There's this intermingling of joy and sorrow, hope and memories, longing and losing.

Ezra says "the people could not distinguish the sound of the *joyful* shouting from the sound of the people's *weeping*."

So it is with us.

The sixth stage of grief is this creativity stage where we can create something new for one another in spite of our grief. It's where we recognize each other's grief and vow to make life a little easier for each other, to show each other that we're not forgotten.

We can laugh and cry.
We can mourn and move forward.
We can grieve and create.

We can hear the cries of a stubborn, old man and tap our feet with joy to his favorite music.

See, the biggest lie we tell each other in our grief is that we have to go through this alone.

But the Church is the place where we show compassion on one another and we prove the existence of God by being the presence of God! We're *never* alone in our grief.

We have a bunch of annoying, crazy, messed up people who haven't forgotten us in our grief!

We still matter.

And the church shows us *life* still matters.

The church reminds us that it's never about those moments of death and darkness. It's about those moments of life and light and laughter.

Life will find a way.

Life is eternal in Jesus Christ and we can always, always, always celebrate these glimpses of life that take our breath away.

These moments where we can't help but grin from ear to ear. *Even at a funeral.*

Thanks be to God.

Chapter 9:
Game Six

Does God answer prayer?

//

It's Game 6 of the World Series on Thursday, Oct. 27, 2011, between the St. Louis Cardinals and the Texas Rangers. The World Series is a series of seven games, where the winning team has to win 4 out of the 7 games. The Rangers are winning the series 3-2, after coming back to tie the series twice, and now they have the lead. One more win to win it all.

The Texas Rangers play in my hometown, Arlington, TX. The Texas Rangers have never won a World Series before. This was their second year in a row to go to the World Series, but they lost badly the previous year to the San Francisco Giants. Now, they are one win away from receiving their *first world series title*.

It felt like this was it. This was the time for history to be made. This World Series win would mean so much to me, my wife, my family & friends, and all the other Texas Rangers fans. It would mean so much to an organization that is constantly ignored by news broadcasters because they don't have the budget like the New York Yankees, the Boston Red Sox, or the Philadelphia Phillies.

It's the top of the 8th inning and the Rangers are up 7-4, after getting 3 runs in the 7th inning.

This is it. My phone was ringing off-the-chain with messages from relatives and friends. "6 more outs!"

We just kept saying "6 more outs!" 6 more outs to win the World Series and see the 1st ever title for the Texas Rangers.

Still, the news broadcasters were only talking about Albert Pujols. "Where is Pujols going to go after this season? This might be Pujols' last time at-bat for the St. Louis Cardinals."

Seriously?! The Rangers are about to get their first World Series title and all you can do is talk about Pujols?! When will the Rangers get some respect?! *C'mon!!*

The Cardinals scored a run in the bottom of the 8th to make it 7-5.

Then in the 9th inning, the Rangers had two outs and two strikes. They were *one strike* away from winning the title.

The Cardinals hit the ball. *One more out. One more catch.* The ball was flying through the air towards the right fielder Nelson Cruz.

The ball flew right above Nelson Cruz's glove… base hit… tie game, 7-7.

This moment will forever be ingrained in my brain.

Extra innings. The Rangers fans would have to wait a little longer.

Then in the top of the 10th inning, my favorite baseball player at the time – Josh Hamilton – came up to bat.

I had met Josh at the playoff game in Tampa earlier that month. I took a picture with him, had him sign a baseball, and I had him sign his book called "Beyond Belief." His book was about his drug and alcohol addiction and how his family and his faith helped him in the road to recovery.

He was a great example of what I liked about many players and members of the Texas Rangers organization. He, like many others, overcame all odds to play the game of baseball. For many of the Rangers players, faith was a big deal to them.

Hamilton talked a lot about the support he received for his road to recovery from the other Rangers' players and coaches in his book, and it made me greatly respect the team even more.

//

At that moment, Josh hadn't hit a home-run in 65 at-bats. He had been struggling with a groin injury that had kept him from playing at full level. Struggling with injuries was a staple of his career.

I predicted in the third inning to my friends that Josh was going to hit a home run. It didn't happen.

But in the 10th inning, it did! Josh hit a two-run homerun to make the game 9-7. Josh reported later that God told him he was going to hit that home run.

You can call Josh crazy for that, but no one can change what the man felt. He reported:

"God didn't say we were going to *win* that game, but he did tell me, 'You haven't hit a home run in a while and you're going to hit one now.'"

In the bottom of the 10th inning, again, we were *one strike* away from winning the World Series, and again, the Cardinals came back to tie it.

When the Rangers didn't score in the top of the 11th inning, I couldn't watch the bottom of the 11th. My adrenaline was going so crazy that I had to take a break.

Then, the inevitable happened.

David Freese of the St. Louis Cardinals hit a home run to win the game for the Cardinals.

The Rangers lost again the next day in Game 7 to lose the series. *No title.*

Just one of the most memorable World Series ever and one of the most memorable Game 6's ever.

Still, I found myself saying to God, "Are you sure this is the way the series is supposed to end?"

God, is this your final answer?

//

When it appears that life isn't going the way we thought it would, does this mean God said "no" to our prayers? Why does God give us one good thing and then follow it up with something terrible? Why is one prayer answered and then one prayer…not…answered?

The bigger question might be, *"Do we really believe God is good?"* I mean, do we?

Do we believe God is truly good?

//

I invested a lot of time and energy into the Rangers that year. I missed probably less than 5 games in 162 games that season.

For what? A ball game?

What does baseball have to do with the Gospel of Jesus Christ?

//

I don't like praying for sports. But I must admit I did a lot of praying during that baseball postseason.

I tried to remain neutral and objective in my prayers.

"God, just help both teams to play with their God-given talent and keep them safe… but please know how much the Texas Rangers fans want a win, okay?"

After the Rangers lost game 6, the next day Shannon and I were just miserable. I talked with three different friends from Texas that day and with each friend the conversation went like this…

"Did you sleep last night?"

"No, you?"

"No."

You would have thought we were grieving over the death of someone we were so miserable.

I said to God after the Cardinals won the World Series, *"God, there better be a Cardinals fan that wanted this just as bad as I did."*

But in the end, it's just baseball, right?

//

For me, I had experienced a lot of tragedy in the last few months and baseball was giving me something to celebrate. I yelled at God when the Rangers were about to lose just like I was yelling at God the day a good friend of ours – Tommy Sims – was being rushed to the hospital early in the morning.

"God, don't let this happen now! God, we just need more time! Just a little more time!"

God, is this really your final answer?!

//

It was five in the morning when Tommy's brother-in-law, Tom, called me to tell me Tommy was in an ambulance on the way to hospital. Tommy died before he made it there. He was 42 years old.

Tommy had lung cancer, although he never smoked a day in his life. He was the strongest man you ever met.

Tommy and I would talk about how silly some unspoken rules were in the church. We dreamed of the day we could all wear shorts and flip flops to church and no one would care.

The first time I met Tommy was at a baseball game he was coaching for his son, Luke. Some church leaders introduced me to Tommy and he asked me to pray for the team before they played their game.

Tommy's wife, Julya, told me he never came to church much before I was their pastor. At the visitation before his memorial service, they wanted to keep his casket closed. When the visitation ended, I asked the funeral director if I could see him to have some closure.

He was wearing his "God is Big Enough" wristband I gave him during a sermon series we did on suffering.

The "God is Big Enough" wristband began at First United Methodist Church in Mansfield, Texas after the pastor's brother also had cancer. It was a symbol of hope and faith in the face of suffering.

Tears began to flow when I saw Tommy wearing this wristband.

As I told Julya how I noticed what he was wearing, she said, "Russell, he wasn't a man of many words. But his faith meant so much to him before he died. He never took that wristband off after you gave it to him."

//

Earlier that season, when the Tampa Bay Rays made it into the playoffs, my dreams were coming true. This meant I was able to attend two playoff games there to see the Texas Rangers win and advance in the playoffs after a very emotional time for Shannon and myself. This was one week after Tommy had passed away.

A little sports team was giving us something to celebrate when we didn't have much to celebrate.

//

Shannon and I had been trying to have our first child. In a span of two years, Shannon had three miscarriages. Hope was all but lost for us.

I had always dreamed of becoming a father. I truly looked forward to sharing my goofy personality with my own child and raising them to see God and God's love story the way I've seen it.

Tommy's brother-in-law, Tom, had grown to be one of my best friends, and his wife, Michelle, had become one of Shannon's closest friends too. They listened to us and cried with us more than anyone during that time.

We didn't know how many people had experienced miscarriages before because no one talks about it. It's too hard to talk about a loss this painful.

Some people say stupid things like, "This happened for a reason," or "God wanted another angel," or "The baby died so something better could happen."

Good-intentioned statements that only entice further pain.

Tom & Michelle Christmas were our true friends who sat in silence with us, just as we did when Tommy died. They didn't try to say "things will get better." They were our family.

They met us in our mess.

//

During this time, the Rangers making the playoffs became more than just baseball. It became a reason to find joy again.

//

A lot of ministers have equated America's passion for sports as something that separates us from passion for God.

I was talking a while back with some minister friends about how soccer has become more important with a lot of families on Sunday mornings than coming to church.

One friend said his senior pastor scared off a lot of people when he said, "If you don't quit taking your kids to play soccer on Sunday mornings, then you don't really care about God."

With the same friends we were talking about how no one questions driving to a football game in the rain, but we use rain as an excuse not to come to church.

I responded, "It's not our passion for sports that is the problem. The problem is when we don't have this same passion for God. Instead of us always criticizing soccer families for not coming to church on Sunday mornings, why don't we, as a church, do something to reach out to *them*? I agree that God and church should receive a higher priority than soccer, but it's not happening. How can we, as a church, help them to be able to make church and God more of a priority? There has to be some sort of "meeting in the middle" balance between a church's commitment to its people and a family's commitment to the church?"

One week I had talked with elementary school kids about how we can "be the church" better.

The kids' suggestions were:

1. We need more candy.
2. We need recycling bins.
3. We need more donuts.
4. We should create a second service for people who can't be here on Sunday mornings.

These kids understood we need to reach out to those who can't be here on Sunday mornings.

Instead of criticizing, we could love people where they are.

Instead of criticizing what people are passionate about, maybe we can help people to see how they can integrate their passion for sports (or music or art or whatever their passion may be) to their passion for God. Maybe we'd see God answering our prayers more often if we could see how God is already moving through our everyday, ordinary circumstances.

How can sports help connect them to God? How can sports bring glory to God? How can sports lead people to pray genuine, passionate prayers that ultimately connect people to God in Jesus in the Holy Spirit? How can this lead people to love people and tell a bigger, more important story than just "sports"?

How can our ordinary passions lead us to more passionate prayers and a passionate life for Christ?

Sports, much like band and dance and other group activities, helps teach teamwork and commitment and endurance. These things can connect us to God's teachings if we're paying attention.

Sports gave me the story of Josh Hamilton and his endurance to fight addictions and rely on his faith.

Sports has highlighted the story of David Murphy, another Rangers outfielder during the 2011 World Series.

Murphy has said, "The game of baseball should be my ministry. My testimony is my life. I pray that I use the talent I've been given to play baseball to bring glory to God."

"I want to be known as David Murphy, all star player or David Murphy, World Series champion, but more importantly, I want to be known as David Murphy, man of God."[57]

//

Sports helped me to connect to other people at the church in Reddick, like 6th grader Noah.

Every time Noah and I would see each other, the first words out of our mouths was something sports-related. Usually one or the other has bragging rights over some game that happened the night before. And the other one makes up some excuse as to why his team lost.

Sports helped connect Noah and me and get our conversations going.

Talking about sports with Noah gave me an escape when I needed it the most.

Before Tommy Sims funeral, I was really nervous about getting too emotional. I wasn't nervous about speaking in front of 400 people. I was more nervous about getting too emotional that I couldn't make it through the service.

Noah may or may not have realized what he was doing, but before the service he sat with me in my office and talked with me about sports. This was just the distraction I needed that I believe truly helped me get through Tommy's service. Noah sitting with me talking about sports helped me out in ways I can never thank him enough for.

//

Sports also helped to unite many of us when we were grieving the loss of Tommy.

When Tommy passed away, we thought it wasn't just a coincidence that the next weekend was the Florida vs. Alabama game. Like I mentioned in Chapter 4, most of the church members in Reddick are Florida Gator fans, but Tommy was an Alabama Crimson Tide fan. Many of us gathered together to tailgate for that game, and that day became so much more than just about a football game. It became a day I will never forget.

In the midst of the moms at tailgating shielding their children's eyes because of some certain kind of "dancing" that was going on and as I was scratching my nose because I was smelling something in the air that I knew wasn't exactly "legal" – in the midst of that, I was having conversations with numerous people talking about their friend, Tommy, and their relationship with God and what they understood from the message I gave at Tommy's service…the message that Noah previously had inadvertently helped me deliver by talking to me about sports.

While we were tailgating at a sports-related event, I was having conversations about *God* and *faith* and *tragedy* and *community* and *friends* and *passion for God* that I will never forget. We held each other, we cried together, we laughed together, we danced together, and this sporting event became so much more than about sports and a passion for sports.

It reflected for me the glory of God. It became about us being there for each other in a time of need. It became about us being a community, a body of Christ, doing exactly what we needed to do for each other in that moment.

That tailgating event became something sacred.

//

Many times sports are not about sports if we're looking at the bigger picture. At the end of a season if it's just about the game, only one team and only one team's fans can truly be happy.

Everyone else is looking forward to the next season. Everyone else is looking forward to a new start.

The Texas Rangers still have not won a World Series.

Yet, the bigger picture is that their 2011 season helped my wife and me to find joy when we needed it most, and that wasn't just baseball. I'm positive God was in there somewhere.

The bigger picture is the distraction of sports helped me to have the courage to share the story of the life of one OWESOME saint.

The bigger picture is a sporting event can unite a community for more than just a "game."

Baseball & tailgating & talking about sports with a 6th grader were all answers to my prayers.

These ordinary circumstances helped connect me to something bigger.

To God and God's glory.

The bigger picture is that the glory of God can take whatever we're passionate about and help create in us a new passion for *Him*.

We just have to open our eyes to see *God's glory* is already inside *our story*.

//

Romans 12:1-2: "Take your everyday, ordinary lives – your sleeping, eating, going to work, and walking around lives – and place it before God as an offering. Embracing what God does for you is the best thing you can do for God."[58]

Chapter 10:
Mud

"You are not doing this to the church property."

"But you don't understand. This will be such a big event for our teens. It will be something we will never forget. And it will make their friends want to come back and see all the fun we're having as a church. I'm begging you, Mr. Rogers!"

"You are not destroying church property to have fun."

We had this large field next to the church that would have been perfect to build a mud pit. I had this dream of holding a Mud Olympics for the teenagers in Reddick. Since I was a teenager, I had been having Mud Olympic events at every church I served. We till up a large piece of field, water it for a day or two, and then there is this nice, squishy, disgusting mud pit.

At the Mud Olympics, we would have different relay races like army crawls, the "lawn mower" where one person holds another person's legs while they walk on their hands, and the crab walk. We would have a mud wrestling tournament for the girls and then the boys. And of course a free-for-all mud throwing time to get everyone as dirty as possible.

Mud would be stuck in your ears and hidden places for weeks.

It was OWESOME!

This would be a fun event encouraging the students to bring their friends. It was a time to get a little dirty and let the students be free to be themselves, to be free to express childlike behavior.

This was part of welcoming the *new generation* into the church. As mentioned in Chapter 3, *2 Chairs,* "the kids were coming back to church." Adults under 50, as well as kids and teenagers, started to see a church that cared for them. We spent time with them. We had fun glorifying God.

One of my favorite moments was leading children's time in my last year in Reddick singing my old youth minister's song, "The Football Song." The entire area in front of the pews was full of children and teenagers. There were about 25+ students singing and dancing, along with the rest of the congregation.

This Mud Olympics would be a big part of welcoming the new generation.

Tom & I presented our intentions to our chair of trustees. The trustees oversee anything having to do with the church property. Steve Rogers, the chair of trustees, quickly shut us down.

"You are not doing this to the church property."

Mr. Rogers would not budge on his decision and we were heartbroken. We explored other ideas but they all came up empty.

All we wanted to do was play in the mud.

//

Mr. Rogers and I clashed often. We once had a 3-hour conversation debating whether technology was good for society or not. My relationship with Mr. Rogers was one of my most important relationships in the church because he challenged me often.

It was part of *bridging the generational gap.*

It was the wonderful problem of helping young and old leaders understand one another. As discussed in Chapter 6, *The Affirmessy Process,* the young leaders had to learn the correct process for running a church and respecting the traditions the older generation valued, while the older leaders learned to be mentors to the younger generation and welcome their excitement to do new things.

While Mr. Rogers hated technology, he and his wife, Cindy, had an excellent idea to bridge the generational gap between our members. He suggested holding a Technology Workshop for a family night event. One Wednesday evening we met to have dinner together, and at dinner we encouraged the younger generations to sit with someone older who they had never sat with before.

Then our teenagers led this Technology Workshop. They taught the older generation how to use their cell phones, Facebook, YouTube, and answer any questions about technology they might have. We had over 75 people in attendance for this workshop. This was perfect because it taught the youth leadership, while also having our teenagers spend quality time with our retired members.

While Mr. Rogers and I disagreed on many issues, we supported one another. I knew he had my back and he knew I had his. He tells me exactly what he feels, we fight about it, and then we support one another despite our differences. We didn't have to agree with one another to truly care for one another and respect one another.

I always want people like that in my corner. His skepticism helped me to push myself often.

I knew Mr. Rogers was going to stick to his guns and he knew I was going to stay true to mine, but we learned so much from each other by getting to know one another's perspectives.

//

When the church leaders started talking about introducing new music to the church, Mr. Rogers was the first to comment, "Well, the church got used to Russell. Surely, we can get used to contemporary music too."

Mr. Rogers had the biggest smile on his face, though, when we started playing The Statler Brothers for Bud to make sure we *don't forget the older generation.*

We made sure to not forget the older generation when we heard the concerns of people like Bud and made them feel valued as they became weary of the growing and changing church around them.

One Sunday at the end of my sermon I asked Gaynelle, one of the oldest members in the church, to dance with me as part of an illustration for my sermon. We danced to Burt Bacharach's "What the World Needs Now" (is love sweet love). We reflected on what it means to get up and dance and show the world we will express God's love no matter the situation. It was one of the sweetest moments I can remember during my time in Reddick and reflected our commitment to honor the older generation in the church.

The same commitment we had for playing in the mud for the teenagers we also had to have for our seasoned members. This included visiting them in their homes and visiting them in the hospital. All it took was sitting down to hear their stories and showing them they are still worth it to the church. Showing them they are still valued and there is a chair at the church for them.

//

When I was mad at Mr. Rogers for not allowing us to build a mud pit at the church, he called me later that week. He asked me to come to his home about a mile away from the church.

He walked me over to the front of his home.

"This is where my garden is going to be. It's just been freshly prepared to plant new flowers and vegetables and the like. *But first it will be the perfect spot for your Mud Olympics.*"

"Are you serious?!"

I thought he had totally rejected the idea. I thought he was being an old grump.

Just when I thought our plans were hopeless, Mr. Rogers surprised me.

"I didn't want to mess up the church property, but I have no problem with the teenagers playing in the mud here at my home."

He opened up his *own home* to do something for our teenagers.

And so we did. We had a blast playing in the mud.

There was no one with a bigger smile on his face during the event than Mr. Rogers.

I was sure to let everyone know to thank him for opening up his home for all of us.

"But maybe don't give him a hug right now while you all are covered in mud."

"Yes, hugs can wait," Mr. Rogers proclaimed with a smile.

This showed me his character and passion for our kids more than anything else he has ever done.

When we needed someone to come through for us, he came through for us.

He literally met us in our mess and played in the mud with us.

//

Mr. Rogers probably taught me more during my time in Reddick than anyone else did. He was so humble. He was our greatest asset, but he would never want to take the credit for it. He did the most to welcome a new generation by sacrificing himself and his own home to spend time with them and do something special for them. Despite his own hatred for technology, he bridged the generational gap by suggesting the technology workshop. He was the first to let me know when the seasoned members needed to feel valued. And it was Mr. Rogers who helped make this church *one generation.*

These were the four stages our little church in Reddick experienced during my 3-year tenure there:

1. Welcoming the new generation
2. Bridging the generational gap
3. Don't forget the older generation
4. Becoming one generation

At the end of my time serving as pastor in Reddick, we became one generation loving each other the way church is supposed to.

//

One of our families was on vacation during spring break when their house went up in flames. A relative went to check on their house only to discover it had been through a massive fire. The television in their teenage daughter's room – we later found out – started the fire. If they had been home and not on vacation, things could have been tragic.

We encouraged the family to enjoy their vacation and we would take care of things for them. Our other families and teenagers on spring break themselves gave up their own time to band together and help clean out one family's home. We were covered in black soot from head to toe and coughing from inhaling the smoke, but we all had a smile on our face helping out a family we considered part of our own family. Those who couldn't be there to help clean out their home were there with cleaning supplies or gifts for the family to help them recover when they returned.

We had a fundraiser for the church. At the church council meeting they voted for 100% of the proceeds from the fundraiser to go towards this family. This church, which had been financially unstable only a few years ago, was able to give so extravagant a gift. OWESOME!

We were able to step up and be the church for them.

As we were cleaning out their home, there was nothing left to clean in the girl's room where the fire started. Her bed was melted down into box springs alone. Her family wanted to find something salvageable to give to her when she returned home. They wanted to show her that all is not lost.

As they dug through her belongs, they found one item. The only item that was left undamaged was the teenage girl's bible she had received at confirmation the previous year.

The bible surviving the fire was a testament to what brought us there. We became one generation to serve a family in need because of the One who saves us from our own fires, the One we read about in that old, old book.

//

Another example of becoming one generation was Tom Christmas' mother, Mama Jo. She served at the Ronald McDonald House every month, she taught Sunday school for our children, she would be Ms. Claus at Christmastime (her last name was Christmas after all), and she was a teacher by profession. During her battle with breast cancer, she continued to do all of this until she was physically unable.

What we loved about Mama Jo was she showed us what Jesus looks like. She met us in our mess and loved us right where we are. She demonstrated for us this unconditional love, empowering strength, and a heart for others. She lived to play in the mud with our kids.

We held a "dance-a-thon" for Kayla, a young adult who had a drunk driver plow directly into her bedroom, and for Mama Jo in her battle with breast cancer. This was our chance as a church to dance for someone who gave up so much for us.

We raised money to help with their medical costs and home needs. It was an OWESOME Sunday when the youth danced down the aisle of the church to raise awareness that they would be "dancing for a difference." They invited everyone in the church to dance with them.

This was *heaven* watching an entire room full of many generations dancing together *at church*.

//

I loved watching this church become one generation.

I loved watching the teenagers run across the entire church to hug their older friend in a wheelchair.

I loved watching the seasoned members sing new songs just as loudly as our children.

I loved when we were able to band together to hold a mission trip in our little town.

//

One of my all-time favorite stories is about a girl named Claire I met on a youth mission trip. When I met Claire she was dressed in all black – black clothes, black hair, black make-up, & a dark, lifeless expression.

I said, "Claire, be happy! We're about to have a fun week!"

"I have no reason to be happy," she replied.

"Claire, *smile!*"

"I have no reason to smile."

As the week progressed, I watched Claire. She started to make new friends. She found joy in helping others rebuild their homes. She found a kitten on her worksite and made a new buddy.

By the end of the week, she was grinning ear-to-ear. You couldn't take her smile away.

Claire became her true self, the person God made her to be.

What I always loved about youth mission trips is something I once heard my friend Sarah's daughter say when she was in 7th grade:

"These trips show us how life should really be."

On these trips, everyone is focused on serving God by serving one another and people in need. Everyone is relaxed and having a great time even when they're in the summer heat working hard most of the day to repair homes. Everyone is digging deeper into who they are and who they are meant to be.

They're focused on how life should really be – and when we do that we can't help but smile.

//

My friend, Aaron, brought his youth group from Texas to conduct a mission trip like this at our church in Florida. This helped our church to see mission trips from two points of view. Our church members in need had the experience of being served. And our teenagers had the experience of serving.

We served our church members in need by doing projects like yard work, painting houses, building wheelchair ramps, repairing rooftops, and rebuilding front porches.

Tom and Julya – who helped the teenagers with their work – said it was the most transformative week of their lives.

Mr. Rogers admitted he never believed we could pull off the mission trip week at the church. It was a large task to complete, including gathering all the lumber and tools needed to do the work and finding cooks and enough food to feed an army and places for our students to shower during the week. It was a monumental task but we did it.

At the conclusion of our mission trip, Mr. Rogers confessed, "You taught me how to have a bigger faith. I didn't believe you could pull that off but you did."

//

We ended up being featured in numerous articles for our mission trip, our ability to bring fun into church, for becoming one generation, and for having the "secret to church growth."

The small, little town of Reddick was featured on the front page of the United Methodist Church website as having the "secret to church growth."[59]

//

When I came to be pastor in Reddick, it was not far from shutting its doors forever. With only a handful of people in worship, what was the point?

There might have only been a handful of people at first, but there were *people*.

With a little compassion, a chair for someone in need, and a chair for a friend, we became a church again.

We learned to have fun while glorifying God.
We opened up our homes to play in the mud.
We found the bible in the fire.
We danced in church.
And we were featured for having the "secret to church growth."

Jim Stroup, the mayor of Reddick and the church's lay leader, said to me on my last Sunday:

"We needed you and you needed us."

When my loser self needed a church to serve and this dying church needed a pastor to truly care for them, we met each other in the mud.

As Eugene Peterson puts it:

"What is the greatest thing about being a pastor? The mess."[60]

//

Some people ask why God doesn't take us out of the mess we're in, but I think it's more meaningful that Jesus doesn't take us out of our mess.

He gave us all our surrogate moms and dads like Mama Jo and Mr. Rogers who embrace the child in us and play in the mud with us.

Jesus came to this earth to be a little child to teach us to love children the same way. For when we do, we experience the kingdom of heaven.

Jesus said in Matthew 18:3-5:

"I tell you the truth, unless you change and become like little children, you will never enter the kingdom of heaven. Therefore, whoever humbles himself like this child is the greatest in the kingdom of heaven. And whoever welcomes a little child like this in my name welcomes me."[61]

True love doesn't take us out of the mud pit; true love plays in the mud with us.

True love empowers us to be OWESOME!

//

When we would say The Apostle's Creed – a statement of our beliefs – every Sunday, I would encourage the church to smile when they read this statement. We're saying what we believe and who we are and we should smile as we say this! It brought me such joy as the church caught on and would make eye contact with me with a big smile on their face as we read "The Apostle's Creed."

On my last Sunday in Reddick, we had to bring in extra chairs to make room for everyone in attendance. The entire church surprised me during the reading of "The Apostle's Creed" that morning.

As we stated what we believe as a church, everyone held up smiley face signs.

The entire church was packed with smiles all around.

Chapter 11:
Ms. Eva

On my last Sunday serving as pastor at First United Methodist Church in Reddick, Ms. Eva Haff couldn't make it to church that Sunday. At the time, Ms. Eva was the oldest living member of this church.

After the service was over and we all took pictures with everyone and ate lunch and said goodbye, Shannon and I went to see Ms. Eva at home.

We visited with her for a while.

We told her we would always treasure the guardian angels she would make for us at Christmas.

I told her to always stay "mean" as she used to love to tell me how mean she was.

One of my favorite memories of Ms. Eva was visiting her on her 96th birthday. I took her a Disney princess balloon and a 6-year old's birthday card, which I had added a 9 in front of. I wanted to make her feel like a kid again. She showed me all the treasures she made in her spare time on that day and told me countless stories from throughout her long life.

As I mentioned in chapter 9, *Game 6*, Shannon had three miscarriages. All of them were during the time I was serving in Reddick.

Shannon was 7 months pregnant at the time we visited Ms. Eva on our last Sunday. This was her fourth pregnancy.

I remember one of the last things Ms. Eva said to us as we hugged her goodbye was that she was praying for our baby *every day*.

//

My mother used to repeatedly tell me a story about a bird.

My parents had three daughters but they always wanted a baby boy. The doctor told them a fourth child was impossible so they gave up hope.

My grandfather – my mom's dad – always wanted them to have a boy too. He passed away a couple years before I was born.

My mother found herself pregnant – and found out it was a boy! She went to tell my grandma the good news but before she could tell her my grandma spoke up:

"You're having a boy!"

"How did you know?"

"A bird knocked on my window and I knew it was your father telling me you're going to have a boy!"

My mom would always tell me this story of a bird knocking on my grandma's window.

There are ten years between my youngest sister and myself. My oldest sister is eighteen years older than me. I often joke with her that she could be my mom too.

My sisters would always tell me I'm the accident. But my mother would always reassure me with the bird story that I'm a miracle.

//

Because of this story I always look at birds like they are saints watching over us.

Whenever I see a bird I think that maybe it is Mama Jo or Tommy Sims or Susan Hess or my mentor, Ken Diehm or stubborn, old Bud.

Or Maybe it's Ms. Eva.

//

A couple months after that meeting with Ms. Eva, when she told me she was praying for our baby every day, my daughter, Kennedy, was born on August 16, 2013 at 1:41pm.

Kayla, Ms. Eva's great granddaughter, contacted me later that afternoon to let me know that Ms. Eva had passed away.

Ms. Eva passed away at noon on August 16, 2013.

Considering the time difference, this would mean Ms. Eva passed away about a few hours before Kennedy was born.

As Shannon and I were talking about everything that evening and adoring our new baby girl, we noticed the nurse watching over us overnight was named, Eva.

Of all the names, it was Eva again watching over our baby girl.

Just like the guardian angels Ms. Eva would give out at Christmas time, it seemed as though Ms. Eva was our own guardian angel.

It seems that through all the miscarriages and asking God, "Why?", *God knew exactly what He was doing.*

Ms. Eva was praying for our baby girl every day. We had our own guardian angel. We had our own little bird paving the way for our miracle.

//

It was not even a week – in fact it was four days after Kennedy was born, when I had the fateful meeting back in Texas. It was then that I decided to walk away from the United Methodist Church.

It was a confusing time because when I was in Reddick enjoying being the pastor there, I only longed to be a father. Then when I became a father, I was no longer a pastor. I never had both.

But my story of loss is also one of gain.

Put another way: when I lost my career, I became a father. I fulfilled that dream.

Now, instead of preaching about empowering women to be OWESOME, now I can *live* what I used to preach. I can show my daughter the joy I experienced growing up. I can be the type of father who raises her to believe in herself. She can see how powerful her mother is. And I can change the stereotypes of men who are not involved fathers to show what it really means to be a man. I can embrace my new role as a stay-at-home dad and be the best parent and husband I can be for my family.

One day when Kennedy feels really down because a bully made her feel less-than and she feels like she is not worth it, I can tell her the story about Ms. Eva. I can tell her about the person who prayed for her every day and became a bird shortly before she was born to always look out for her. I can tell her she's a miracle, like my mom used to tell me.

My daughter can hear the story about when I was growing up being bullied and I learned to use what I experienced to help others who are being bullied, to become a minister for the outcasts and losers like me. She can know that while others made me lose confidence in myself, God always taught me something different. That who I am and who she is are both someone created to do great things. We are beloved.

My daughter can hear the story about Susan Hess and Mama Jo and Tommy Sims dealing with cancer. She can hear about how they found strength in their faith to continue to serve others in any way they could.

She can hear about those who lost their lives but their legacies still bring us joy today as we remember their stories. She can know that while we grieve we remember the moments that brought us true joy. We lose our lives but we always have love that gives us new life.

She can hear about all the churches who loved her father and allowed him to use his gifts and taught him to be himself, who God made him to be. And how she can have this same experience in the church.

She can hear about the small, little church in Reddick who became one of the greatest churches I have ever witnessed. While some churches and ministers and congregations are forgetting who they are and who they are supposed to be, there is light and hope in small towns and in small churches. These hidden beacons of light reflect the true light of the world.

She can hear about how life took an unexpected turn for me when I left the ministry. But she was the one who changed my life and gave me hope during that time. She was the answer to my prayers. She was my miracle. She was my new purpose when life threw me a curveball.

And I will always treasure those moments I had with her in the early stages of her life.

She can know that when life takes an unexpected turn for her, which it will, a rainbow is always on the other side of her storms.

She can hear how God made her to be OWESOME and how no one can take away the fact that she is God's child created for a purpose.

Then she can know that purpose is to empower others to tell this story. For those who are told they can't be this or can't be that, to know they matter. They deserve this grace and love and hope and joy just like anybody else.

We can dream of a church and a world and a family that sees who they are. They can see the new, true story that's about them.

It's a new story for today, but it's also an old, old story.

My daughter can be a new bible for today. She can live out the stories in scripture. For God is not to be held in a book. God is progressing his story forward. God is urging us to tell a new story for today.

Scripture isn't scripture if it puts people in a box. The stories in scripture were told for their time to lead us to tell a new story in our time.

The Gospel – the good news – is freeing people to be who they are meant to be today.

It's freeing people from their sin.
It's freeing people from their stereotypes.
It's freeing people from their condemnation.
It's freeing people from their pain, their brokenness.

It's freeing people to be God's children. To know their God-given worth and their God-cultivated confidence.

From a story telling them they're losers – condemned to be outside the church – to finding a place to call home, where outcasts like them know they're OWESOME. They're free to be who they already are in Christ.

They were lost and now they're found.

They have found the new story that reads: "God is not boring! God is exciting!"

God is still moving mountains.

He sees the cries of the needy and the pain of injustice all around us. He meets us in our mess and plays in the mud with us.

God shows us grace. We receive a gift we don't deserve. When we've messed up, there is still hope. No matter who we are, there is still love and grace and hope for us.

God is telling a new story. One where we are "more than C's." One where representation matters. One where anyone is welcome in the church. One where everyone has someone to sit with.

One where God loves us right where we are. *In a chair the Carpenter made just for us.*

Shannon and I pray every night that Kennedy will know *she can be anyone she wants to be – and we will love her no matter who she becomes.*

Everyone needs to know this story is their story.
God's story is *their* story.

We can experience this story on earth just as it is in heaven.

God's story is my story.
God's story is my daughter's story.
God's story is your story.

Like the birds flying in the wind,
Like the saints looking over us,
We can be free to tell this story.

"Amazing grace. How sweet the sound.
That saved a wretch like me.
I once was lost, but now I'm found.
I was blind, but now I see."[62]

Your story of loss is not the end.

There is also something to find.

Now, *that's* a story worth telling.

For Shannon, for always empowering me to be who God calls me to be.

For Kennedy, for being the answer to our prayers.

For those in the mud, for creating a space for all of us to become one generation.

For the saints who have gone on before us, for inspiring us still today.

I'm so excited to tell your story.

NOTES

Chapter 1: Left Out

1. From *X-men: First Class*. Matthew Vaughn. Twentieth Century Fox, 2011. Film.
2. From *Orange is the New Black,* Season 2, Episode 11 "Take a Break From Your Values." Netflix, 2014. Television.
3. Lee, Stan and Kirby, Jack. *The Incredible Hulk.* May 1962. Marvel Comics. New York City.
4-7. *The Holy Bible: New International Version.* Zondervan: Grand Rapids, 2002.
8. Lee, Stan and Kirby, Jack. *The Incredible Hulk.* May 1962. Marvel Comics. New York City.
9. Nietzsche, Friedrich. *"Beyond Good and Evil." The Complete Works of Friedrich Nietzsche.* Gadow Press, 2008. First Published in 1909.
10. From *X-men: First Class*. Matthew Vaughn. Twentieth Century Fox, 2011. Film.
11. Augustine of Hippo. This was quoted in *Spirituality and Liberation: Overcoming the Great Fallacy* by Robert McAfee Brown, p. 136.
12. Matthew 5:44. *The Holy Bible.*
13. "The arc of the moral universe is long, but it bends toward justice." – Martin Luther King, Jr. // This famous quote was paraphrased from a Unitarian minister Theodore Parker from his sermon titled "Of Justice and the Conscience" which was published in his 1853 collection of "Ten Sermons of Religion."
14. Dr. Joretta Marshall is the Dean of Brite Divinity School, Ft. Worth, Texas. She said this in her class on Forgiveness at Brite in 2009.
15. *The Avengers.* Joss Whedon. Walt Disney Studios Motion Pictures, 2012. Film.
16. www.itgetsbetter.org
17. *The Matrix.* The Wachowski Brothers. Warner Brothers Studios, 1999. Film.
18. *The Holy Bible: New International Version.* Zondervan: Grand Rapids, 2002.
19. Clark, Russell. "Why I Want to Be a Christian." Trinity United Methodist Church, 1994. Essay.

Chapter 2: The Dying Church & The Spiky-haired Pastor

20. http://www.umc.org/news-and-media/church-vitality-what-is-the-secret-to-growth#.WdUMO59GXnw.email

21. 1 Samuel 17. *The Holy Bible: New International Version.* Zondervan: Grand Rapids, 2002.

22. *The Holy Bible: New International Version.* Zondervan: Grand Rapids, 2002.

23. Peterson, Eugene H. *The Message Remix: The Bible in Contemporary Language.* NavPress Publishing: Colorado Springs, 2003.

Chapter 3: 2 Chairs

24. *Up.* Peter Docter and Bob Peterson. Walt Disney Studios Motion Pictures, 2009. Film.

25. Emmit Smith. NFL Hall of Fame Speech. Canton, Ohio, 2010. https://youtu.be/zHVAfLIwqGk

Chapter 4: OWESOME

26. Tebow, Timothy R. *Through My Eyes.* HarperCollins: New York, 2011.

27. *The Holy Bible: New International Version.* Zondervan: Grand Rapids, 2002.

28. Kinnaman, David & Lyons, Gabe. *Unchristian: What a New Generation Really Thinks About Christianity.* Baker Books: Grand Rapids, 2007.

29. *The Holy Bible: New International Version.* Zondervan: Grand Rapids, 2002.

30. *13 Reasons Why.* Netflix, 2017. Television.

31. This quote from Mahatma Gandhi is said to have come from a conversation with Christian Missionary E. Stanley Jones in c. 1948.

32. *Inside Out.* Peter Docter and Ronnie Del Carmen. Walt Disney Studios Motion Pictures, 2015. Film.

33. *The Holy Bible: New International Version.* Zondervan: Grand Rapids, 2002.

34. Bell, Rob. *Nooma Sunday 004.* Zondervan: Grand Rapids, 2005. Video.

35. Peterson, Eugene H. *The Message Remix: The Bible in Contemporary Language.* NavPress Publishing: Colorado Springs, 2003.
36. Miller, Donald. *Blue Like Jazz.* Thomas Nelson: Colorado Springs, 2003.

Chapter 5: Reading Day

37. Williamson, Marianne. *"Dream of This." A Return to Love: Reflections on the Principles of "A Course in Miracles."* Harper One: San Francisco, 1992.
38. Peterson, Eugene H. *The Message Remix: The Bible in Contemporary Language.* NavPress Publishing: Colorado Springs, 2003.

Chapter 6: The Affirmessy Process

39. Luke 22: 7-23. *The Holy Bible.*
40. *The Jerk.* Carl Reiner. Universal Pictures, 1979. Film.
41. "Failure to Excommunicate." Album: *The Anatomy of the Tongue in Cheek.* Band: Relient K. Gotee Records, 2001. Song.

Chapter 7: The Mutant Problem

42. This chapter was inspired by Dr. Russell Dalton's book *Marvelous Myths: Marvel Superherous and Everyday Faith,* Chapter 4: "The Uncanny X-men: Dealing with Discrimination and Diversity." Chalice Press: St. Louis, 2011.
43. *X-men.* Bryan Singer. 20th Century Fox, 2000. Film.
44. *X2: X-men United.* Bryan Singer. 20th Century Fox, 2003.
45. Kinnaman, David & Lyons, Gabe. *Unchristian: What a New Generation Really Thinks About Christianity.* Baker Books: Grand Rapids, 2007.
46. Andrew Greer is an author and singer/songwriter/producer. He received a Dove award nomination for his instrumental album *All Things Bright and Beautiful: Hymns for the Seasons.* He is the author of multiple books such as *Winds of Heaven, Stuff of Earth: Spiritual Conversations Inspired by the Life & Lyrics of Rich Mullins* and *Transcending Mysteries: Who is God and What Does He Want From Us?*
47. Lamott, Anne. *Traveling Mercies: Some Thoughts on Faith.* Anchor Books: New York, 1999.
48. John 21:15-17. *The Holy Bible.*

49. Lee, Stan. *Stan's Soapbox: The Collection.* Marvel: New York, 2008.
50. Luke 24:1-2. *The Holy Bible.*
51. Daniels, Lillian. *When Spiritual But Not Religious is Not Enough.* Jericho Books: New York, 2013.
52. *X2: X-men United.* Bryan Singer. 20th Century Fox, 2003.
53. Galatians 3:28. *The Holy Bible.*

Chapter 8: Bud
54. My late mentor, Dr. Ken Diehm, said this to me often.
55. *Duck Dynasty.* A&E. Television.
56. Ezra 3:10-13

Chapter 9: Game 6
57. This was from an inspirational interview of David Murphy for www.iamsecond.com.
58. Peterson, Eugene H. *The Message Remix: The Bible in Contemporary Language.* NavPress Publishing: Colorado Springs, 2003.

Chapter 10: Mud
59. http://www.umc.org/news-and-media/church-vitality-what-is-the-secret-to-growth#.WdUMO59GXnw.email
60. Peterson, Eugene H. *Pastor: A Memoir.* Harper Collins: New York, 2011.
61. *The Holy Bible: New International Version.* Zondervan: Grand Rapids, 2002.

Chapter 11: Ms. Eva
62. "Amazing Grace." Lyrics by John Newton. 1779. Song.

Acknowledgments

A big thank you to all those who took the time to give me feedback and support on my first book and walk with me on this affirmessy journey called life:

John Lee, for creating the cover design and for turning in the guys who stole my clarinet in junior high.

Greg Gruzalski, for reading this story from a complete stranger to give me a fresh, unknown perspective of my book. And thanks to *Brett and Mary Hutson* for getting us connected.

Jim Reeves, for your endorsement and great feedback and for being the voice of reason putting things into perspective in the sports world for so many years.

Jo Lillard, for reminding me of who I am.

Andrew Greer, for always having deep, theological, raw, authentic conversations with me.

Dr. Stephen Sprinkle, for teaching me to be who God calls me to be and for showing me God's kingdom is full of beautiful, gay rainbows.

Dr. Joretta Marshall, for teaching me about forgiveness when I was full of anger and for supporting my journey even after seminary.

Lisa McCulloch for your diligent grammar work and being one of my biggest cheerleaders.

Steve & Cindy Rogers, for making me follow the rules.

Jim Stroup, for telling me to break those rules.

Paul and Victoria Archibald, for being the best friends we were never supposed to have – and are still best friends to Shannon and I today.

The people of First United Methodist Church in Reddick, for being the smallest church in the smallest town with the warmest heart, the greatest witness, the longest tradition, and the biggest story all other big powerful churches should pay attention to.

To all the pastors, youth ministers, church members, mission trip participants, seminarians, theologians, classmates, and friends Shannon and I have had throughout our lives and our time in ministry, thank you for being a part of this journey with us and for being a beacon of God's love.

Tina Price, Lynn Lemon, & Richard Michener, for always allowing me to vent to you my frustrations and celebrations during this writing process – and throughout my life.

Joe Carmichael, for sitting with me in my mess and really listening to my story. Thank you for being the Church for me when I needed a pastor, a mentor, and a friend at my weakest time.

Tom Christmas. When I needed a friend and confidant as a pastor in a new state where I knew nobody, my wife forced me to call you – a church member who I had an immediate bond with – even though pastors are not supposed to be BFFs with church members. Who knew that you, *Michelle, Julya, Tammi, Will, Drake, Brice, Luke, David, Dale, Glen,* and all of your family would create a bond together with our family as strong – or sometimes stronger – than family? You & Michelle have been there for Shannon & I when we needed someone to cry with us the most. We love the Christmas family beyond words and we will always be your family. *#ChristmasStrong #CancerSucks*

My family – Gil, Mary, Kip, Lynn, Trish, Melony, Keith, Kim, Kyle, Tina, Chad, Kacie, Chris, Valerie, Jen, Tony, Kolby, Bridgette, Kory, Kiara, Michael, Alicia, Blake, Shelby, Rylee, Reese, Brandon, Isabelle, Skyler, Preston, Bennett, and all our extended family, for being the place we call home whenever we are with you.

My parents – Gil and Mary Clark, for always supporting me in everything I do, for being the very first to show me what God's love and grace look like, for forcing me to go to church until I couldn't wait to go, and for always reminding me that I'm the miracle, not the accident.

My daughter – Kennedy Clark, for being my joy, for teaching me all over again what God's love and grace and kindness are by your pure, thoughtful heart, and for calling me daddy.

My wife – Shannon Clark, for being my rock, the love of my life, my best friend, for believing in me when I didn't believe in myself, for being a creative artist and OCD clean freak like me, for being a hard-working hot mama and always making your trophy husband feel special, for being the loudest Texas A&M Aggies, Texas Rangers, and Dallas Cowboys fan along with me, and for not allowing me to pursue a "job" but to only do what I *love.* I love you my flippin' hot wife, my sweet Lemon.

About the Author

Russell Clark is a first-time author currently residing in Lexington, Kentucky with his wife, Shannon, and daughter, Kennedy. He graduated with a Masters of Divinity from Brite Divinity School in Fort Worth, Texas and a Bachelor's Degree in Christian Education from Texas Wesleyan University in Fort Worth, Texas. He plans to write his next book about his experiences being a stay-at-home dad to be released late 2018.

Customer Review and Social Media

Please take the time to rate *Loser* and share your thoughts on Amazon. My hope is this book will be helpful to many people. If you feel the same way, please share your thoughts on social media and share this book with 1000 of your closest friends.

Connect

Facebook: fb.me/russellclarkauthor
E-mail: russellclarkauthor@yahoo.com

Booking Information

To book Russell for speaking engagements, please contact russellclarkauthor@yahoo.com. Russell is available to speak at churches, schools, or groups on a variety of topics, such as bullies, empowerment, church leadership, and/or evangelism.

57488393R00095

Made in the USA
San Bernardino, CA
20 November 2017